Seeing into darkness is clarity
Knowing how to yield is strength
Use our own light
and return to the source of light
This is called practicing eternity

–Lao Tzu

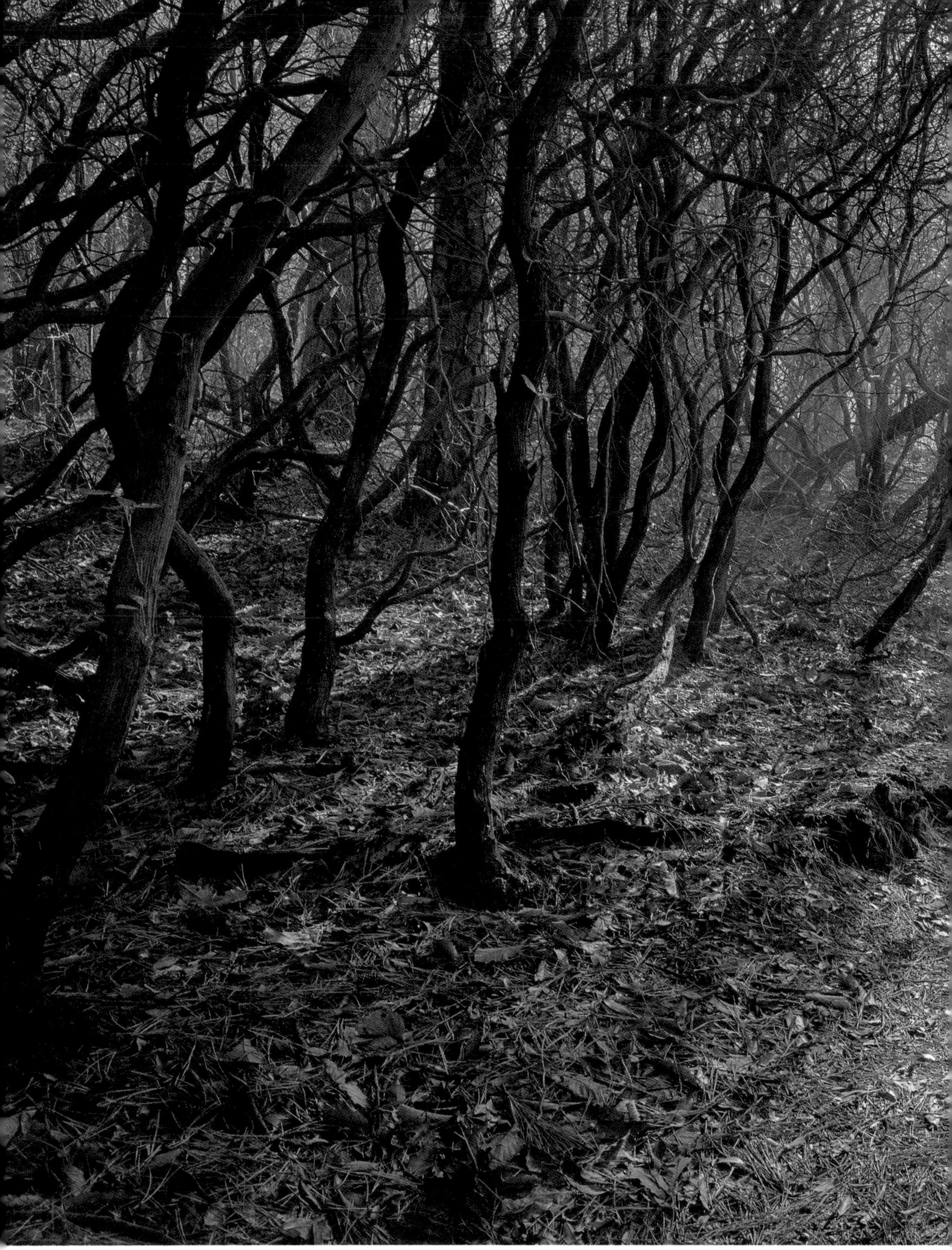

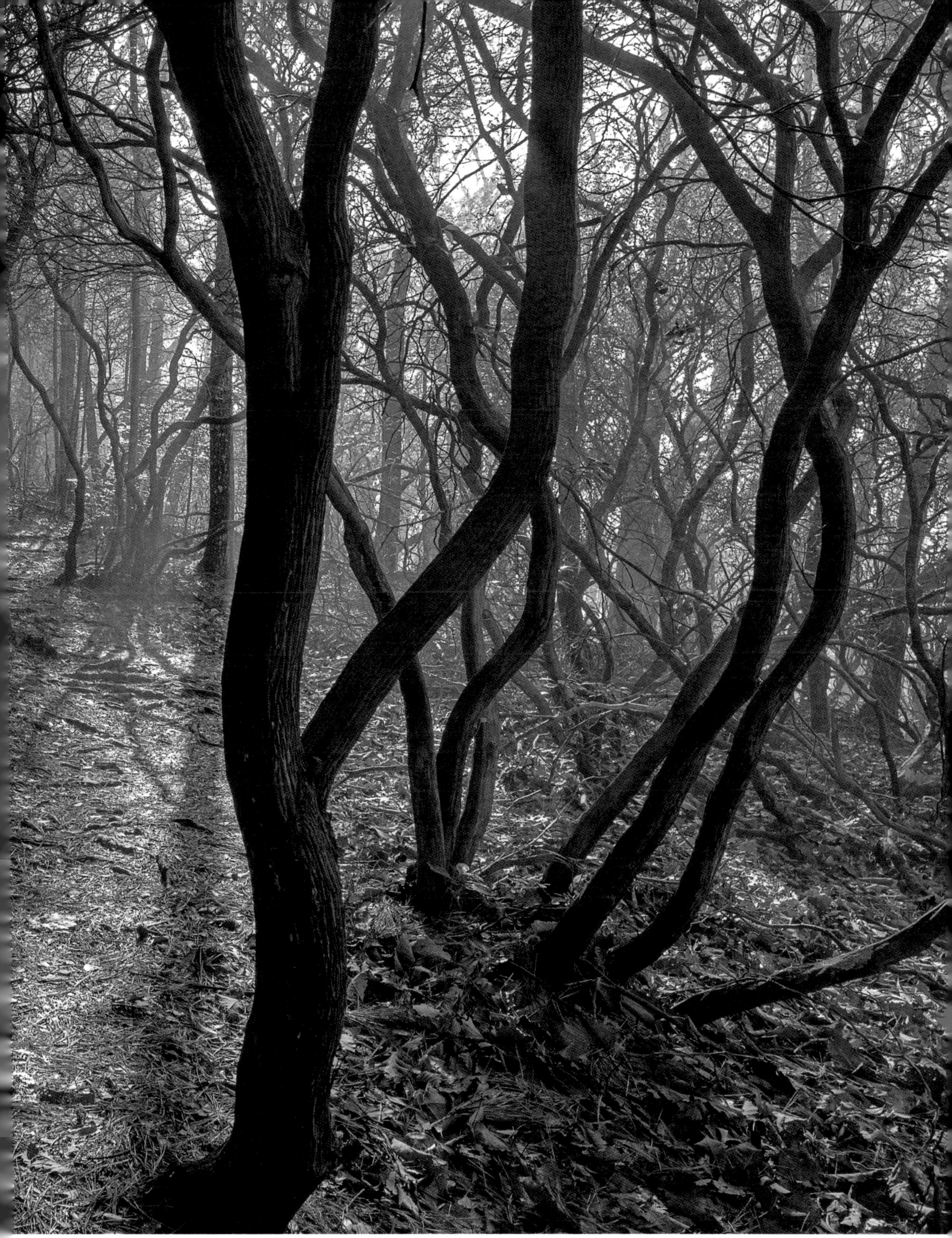

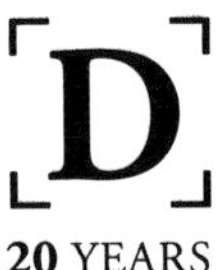

20 YEARS

Cofounders: Taj Forer and Michael Itkoff
Creative Director: Ursula Damm
Copy Editor: Gabrielle Fastman

ISBN: 978-1-9541192-3-9

Printed by Ofset Yapimevi, Turkey

Daylight Books
E-mail: info@daylightbooks.org
Web: www.daylightbooks.org

THE POETRY OF BEING

Photographs and Poems by Lynne Buchanan

To my mother, Barbara Berggren,
who taught me to love nature and poetry,
and to Gaia for providing a beautiful
home for us to explore and learn from
during our time on earth

Introduction

"In a murderous time
       the heart breaks and breaks
           and lives by breaking.
It is necessary to go
       through dark and deeper dark
           and not to turn.
I am looking for the trail.
       Where is my testing-tree?
           Give me back my stones!"

—From "The Testing-Tree" by Stanley Kunitz

I am looking at silence. You know that looking at something also suggests looking from somewhere, from some singular viewpoint. However, in my case, my looking at silence is not just from one but at least two places, and now that you know this, it may also include a third. The silence is the sound of absence. Our absence, mine, yours, even this book's absence. A complete and utterly devastating vacuum. Yet, this negative place suggests the opposite: silence as the sound of wholeness. Our presence, here, full and complete, melds us, the book, its images, the landscapes, the trees and light and rock, into an ageless mush. The act of looking does not just wash over our visual senses but also into the auditory, tactile, olfactory, gustatory, and other senses yet to be named. We look beyond this spread of pages, images, and words. We align light and dark and shades in between with silence. As we look, and forget that we look, we equate absences with timelessness. We arrive at an edge. We begin to revel in insignificance.

Further along in this book, Lynne Buchanan writes, "Ancient faces emerge / In a totem carved by insects / History repeats." Near these words, the photograph titled *Vertical Rock with Holes, Red River Geological Area*. We are pulled to the light-encircled infinities of black. To be tuned up to an edge, up to a featureless darkness, is horrifying—until the moment that we let go of our humanness, our fear of the unknown, our finite selves. That is the nature of attraction, this strange thing in us that defies our baser selves, that lets us look into vacuums, at our insignificance, at our blinking existence.

The phrase about the moth and the flame stands for fatal attractions. It does not consider why moths are drawn to light, and why attraction is a generative process. For this, there may be a better analogy waiting to be coined, such as when flames are placed next to each other. They lean into the other, and are drawn together by forces that are less visible than light, than the flames themselves. Vortices of heated air make them flicker and dance with each other because, as we often tell ourselves, nature abhors a vacuum. Attraction is no longer fatal, and the shifted analogy suggests that we are all like dancing flames in an otherwise invisible greater dance. And then, there's the assumption that Nature rushes in to fill the vacuum; it seems less out of abhorrence and more that the vacuum is Nature's engine. It may be more accurate to say that Nature is Flow: edgeless, constant, churning; where visible and less visible are not just absorbed by all our senses but rather that our senses are part of this vacuum-unvacuum; where the most essential part of being conscious is to be in a state of attraction.

I learned how to light coal fires in Orkney, a fertile archipelago off the north coast of the larger island of Scotland, England, and Wales. Orkney winters can feel bitterly cold because of the islands' full exposure to Atlantic winds. Thankfully, my little cottage had an arrangement that combined a cookstove, fireplace, radiators, and hot water tank into a single, efficient system—but it was heated entirely by fossil fuels. Knowing how to make these lumps of stone and earth flame up and then to keep them burning all day and through the night became a matter of survival. I did not think, staring into the taunting darkness of a small lump of coal, that it was formed from perhaps twenty feet of decaying forest. Nor did I think of the massive weight and the unique conditions (the specifics of which continue to be debated by experts) that compressed hundreds and thousands of feet of decaying material, layer on layer, millennia upon millennia, to render this rock. I did not think about the miners, their horrific working conditions, or their endurance. I certainly did not think enough about the billowing environmental catastrophe that we now live in.

I did not think, back then in 1984, of the eye-blink that humankind has been on this planet: that we have been around for less than 0.018% of the time it took to form the coal that was burning in my fireplace. The vegetation from which coal was formed grew between 359 million years ago and 299 million years ago. We (behaviorally modern Homo sapiens) evolved around 60,000 years ago. It is this, sadly, that brings us to yet another place from which we may look at silence. Our planet may not be anywhere near as fragile as our presence on it. And our existence may have little consequence for this planet 300 million years from now. We are left, then, with how to reconcile our specificity and the cosmos.

Lynne Buchanan's photographs and writing enfold us in a state of attraction, a necessary dynamic, so that we may look at faces more ancient and more persistent than ourselves. The photographs help us grow, become wakeful, and discover our bodily selves in terms of the timeless. This is me reaching out, touching my mother's face, and holding my father's hand. Me, lying on the forest floor, with time to stare up, finding roses in the Milky Way. Reaching for the light, as in the photograph by that title (page 110), argues for this becoming that. More importantly and subtly, the photograph posits that becoming does not necessarily render a transformation, but more a unification. In *Reaching for the Light*, it is the darkness, the seeming lack of information, of material existence, that actually binds the small-leafed plant to the larger one. We lean towards associating darkness with terror. It is the familiarity of leaves and plants that prepare and steady us to look into the tonal depths of this infinity and to stay with it and see through it. Henry Purcell comes to mind for more than one reason here. In the late seventeenth century, he wrote (the text in collaboration with Nathaniel Lee) a song as incidental music to John Dryden's play *Oedipus: A Tragedy*, "Music for a While." The lyrics are troubling at first glance, but the music entices us, along with the opening line and title, to look full in the face of what may scare us, and then to look again, bravely, and then to pass through it, transformed and stronger.

> *Music for a while*
> *Shall all your cares beguile:*
> *Wond'ring how your pains were eas'd*
> *And disdaining to be pleas'd*
> *Till Alecto free the dead*
> *From their eternal bands*
> *Till the snakes drop from her head*
> *And the whip from out her hands.*

The spelling of the original title is "Musick for awhile." As we look back on that last word, the double play of "while" stretches our attention between just a short moment and a much more amorphous period. Stay a while, or awhile. As in the tension between Purcell's lilting, lovely music and the words, there is a tension within each of the different places from which we look at Lynne's photographs, at the silence. Or perhaps it is clearer to think of this tension as attraction. We are attracted to look at the unknown, the undefined, the ambiguous, because it is the key to understanding the relationship between our specific humanness and the cosmos. We are drawn to the edges of no information, of the vacuum, the silence, because that *is nature*: to be in *a traction*. Thus, here, in these pages, the attraction between the words and images, the way they generate a particular silence, provides us with an important reason for looking at Lynne Buchanan's book. The collection helps us reconcile ourselves.

When faced with even the possibility of the infinite or our insignificance, the possibility that our nature may be indelibly destructive, or the possibility that sin equals being human, we respond with varying degrees of terror, fear, and denial. I believe that Lynne Buchanan subscribes, as do I, to Elaine Scarry's remarkable credo, which began as a thought experiment in her book *On Beauty and Being Just* (Princeton, 1999). Scarry notes that beauty, or more precisely, the experience of the beautiful, reminds us of our greatest aspirations and best aspects; the experience of the beautiful orients us towards ideal ways of being, and provides us with a deep keel to help us endure turbulent times. The experience of the beautiful helps us consider, wide with wonder, what we would otherwise avert our eyes from. It is important to note that Scarry brings our attention to the experience rather than the object. Thus, the beautiful is a process, and one of attraction. The experience of looking, as in *The Poetry of Being*, is compelling. It holds our attention so that we may contemplate and stay with silence, solitude, mortality, and chaos, all of which would otherwise leave us feeling fragile, vulnerable, and hopeless. To be attracted here is to take a step towards hope.

—Pradip Malde
Sewanee, Tennessee, 2022

ZEN FOREST

Sun enters the Zen forest.
Still.
Cool.
No hurry.
Only questions:
Really, who are you?
Really, why is that
white pine?

—James P. Lenfestey

THE WHITE PINE'S ANSWER

Distant caws.

And the unspeakable delicacy
of needles stirred by sunlight.

And broom fingers reach
toward the red squirrel's tender leap.

Above me, black embracing arms.
Below, five thighs
with a grip more fierce
than a hundred human lives.

Saying, lie down.
Here, rest.
Here everyone listens.

—James P. Lenfestey

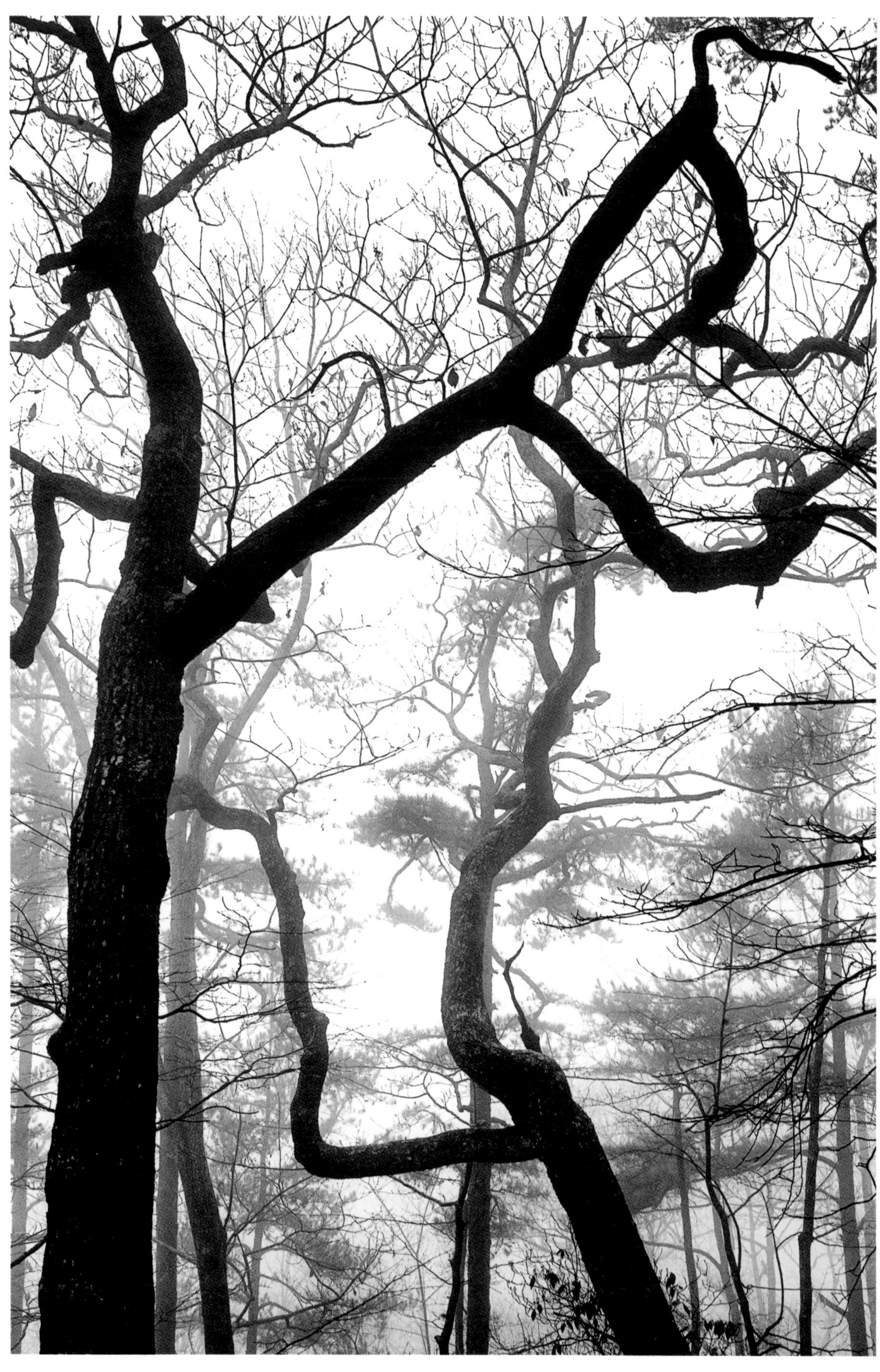

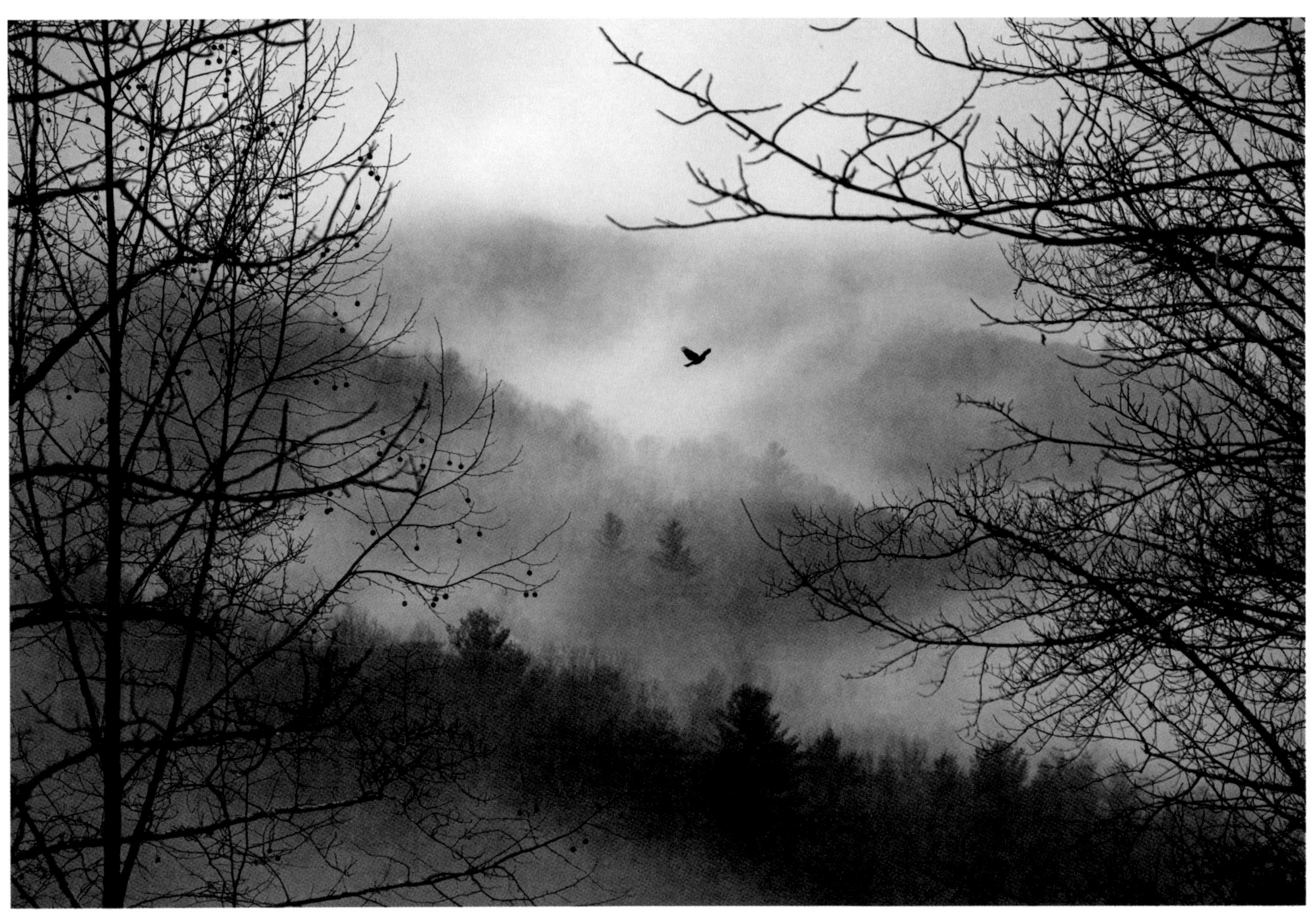

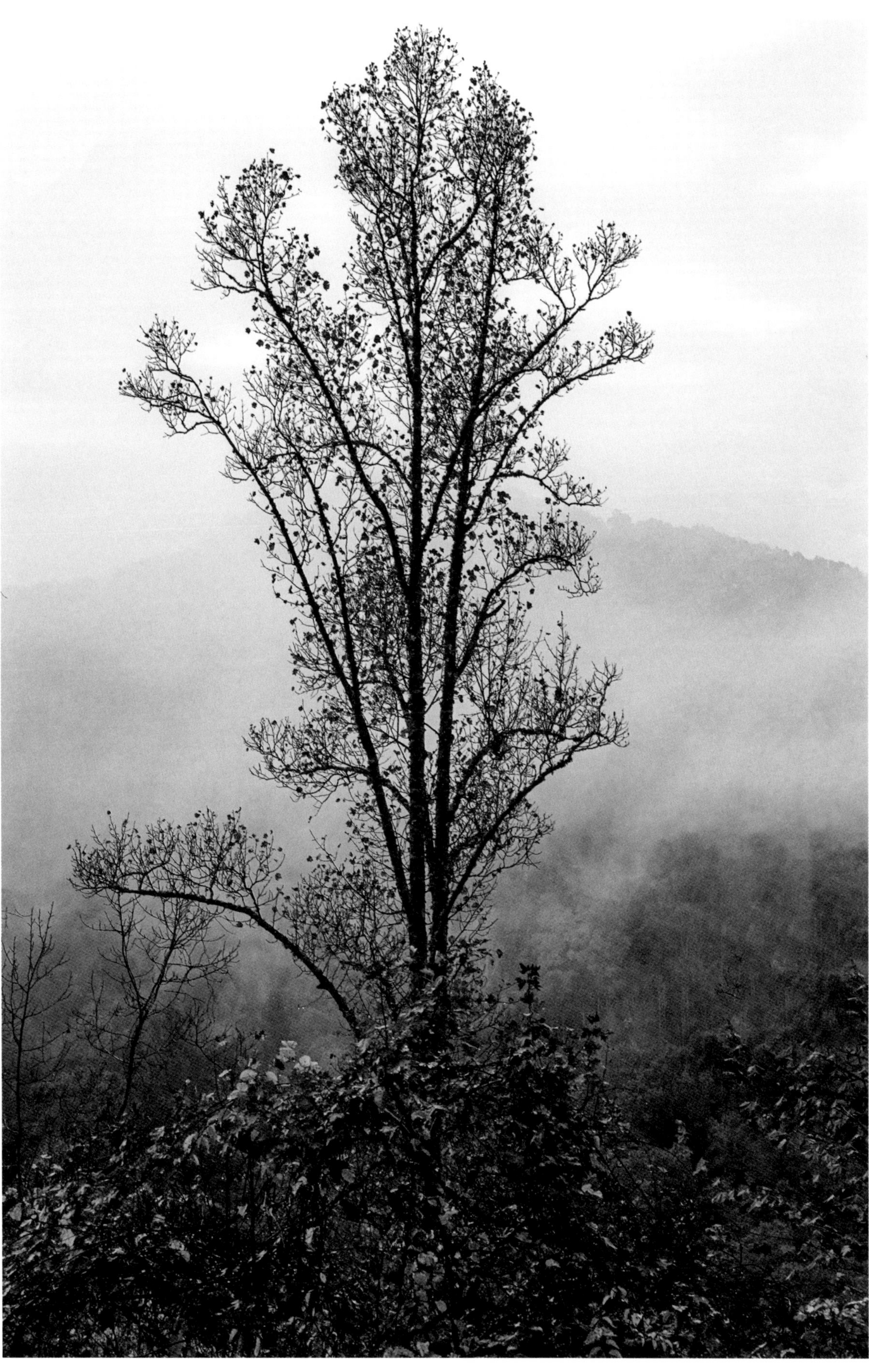

Dancing within veils
Life's eternal energy
Shines as it transforms

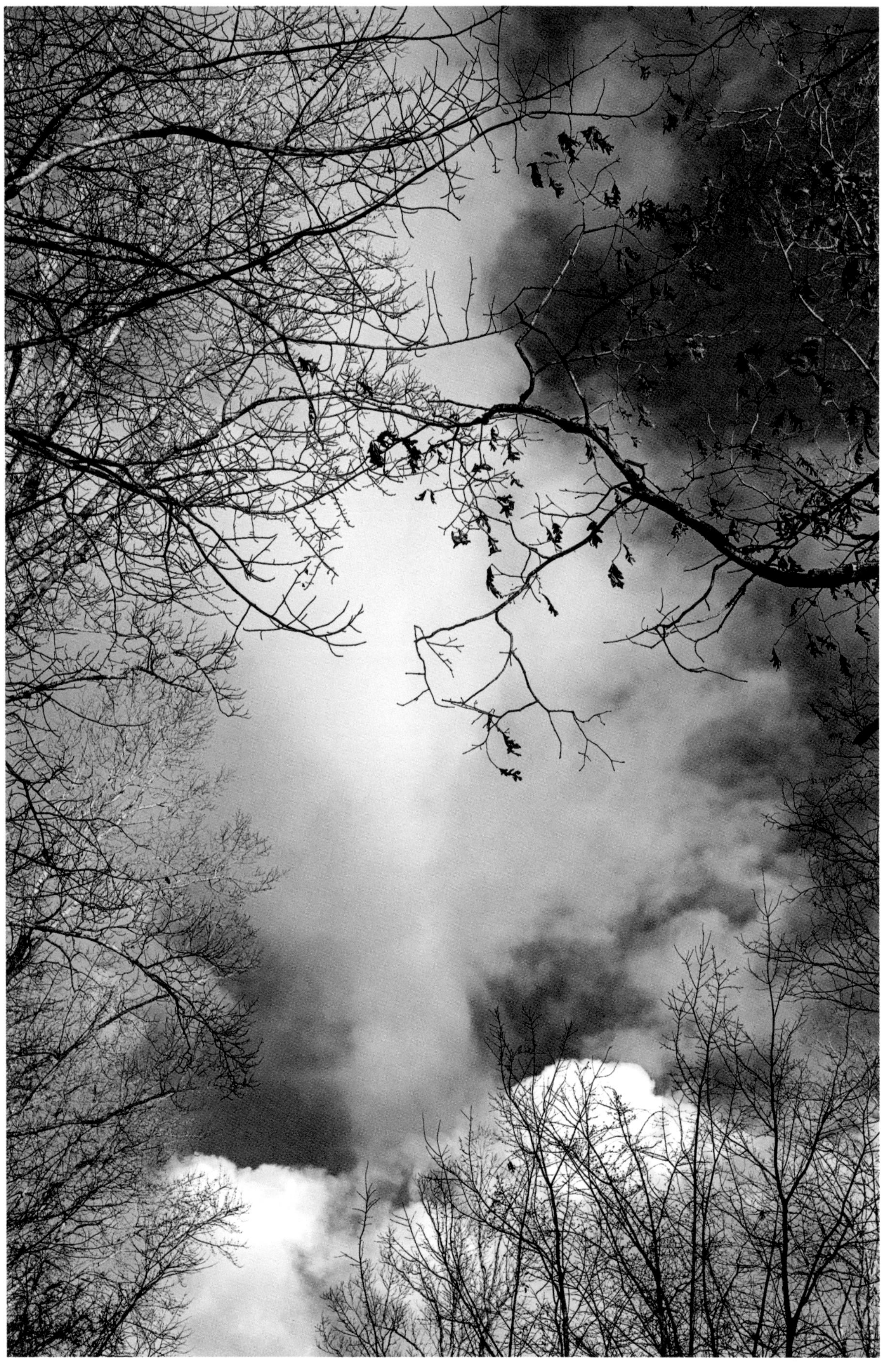

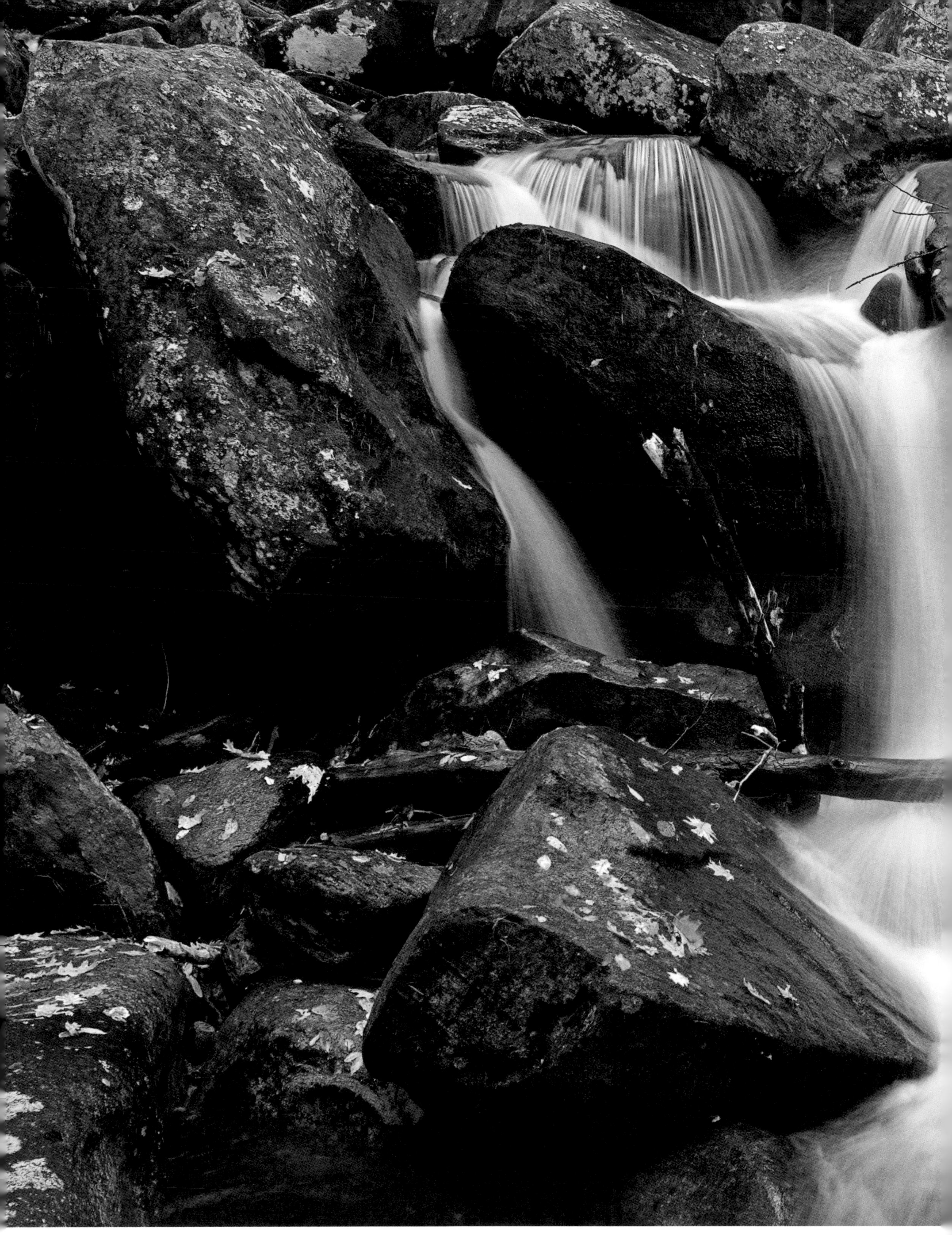

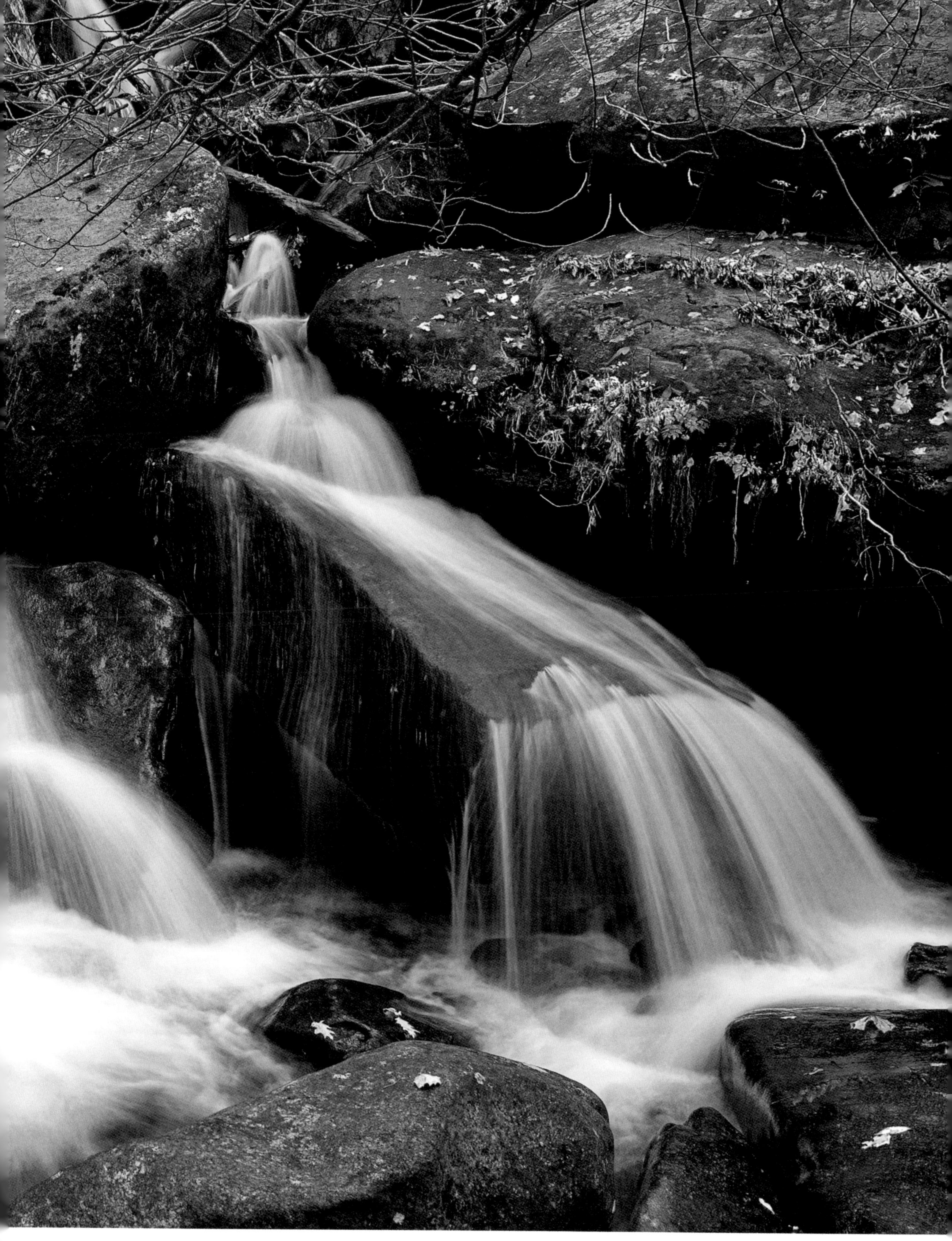

On a hot summer's day
Dancing droplets of water
Revive body and soul

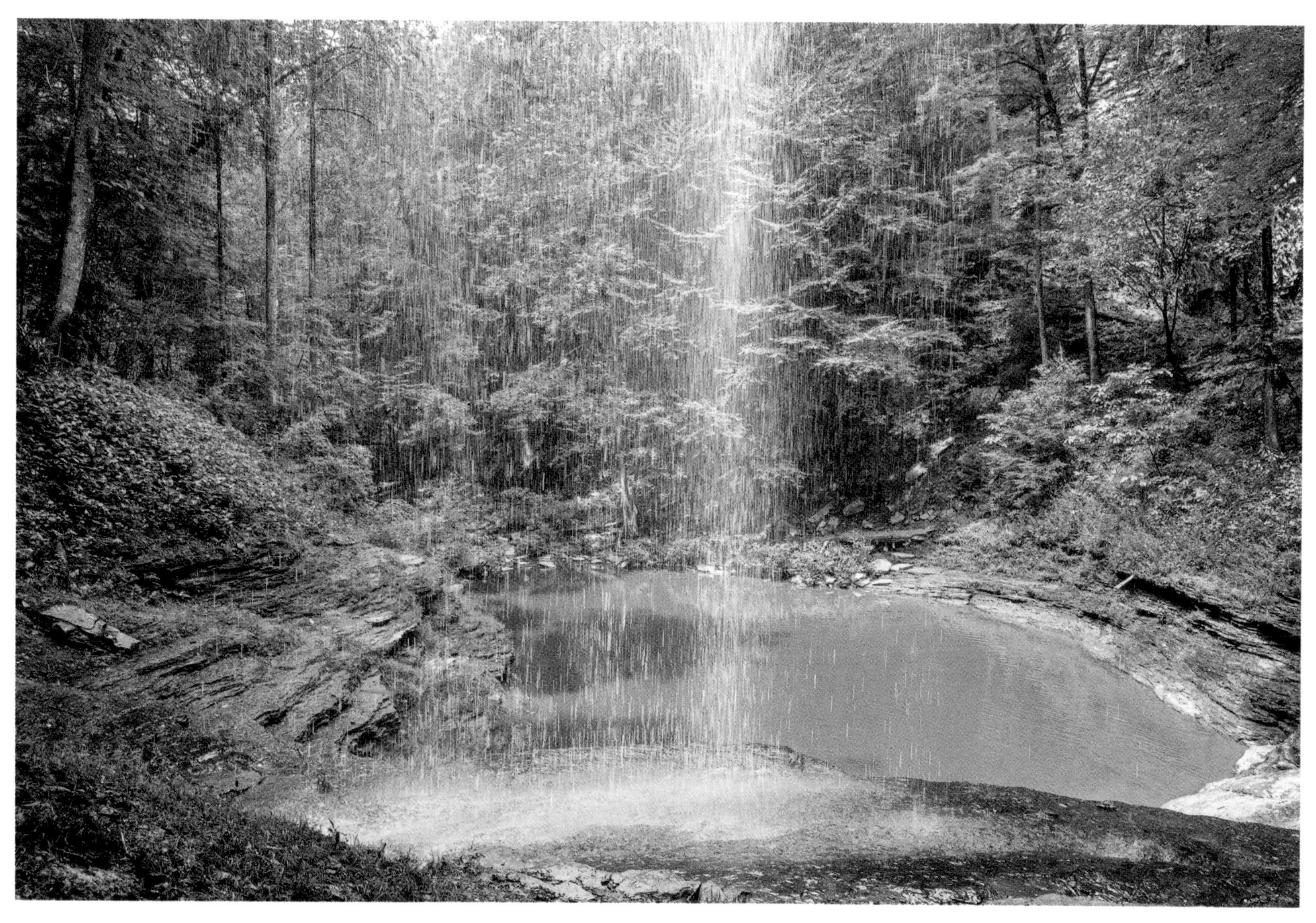

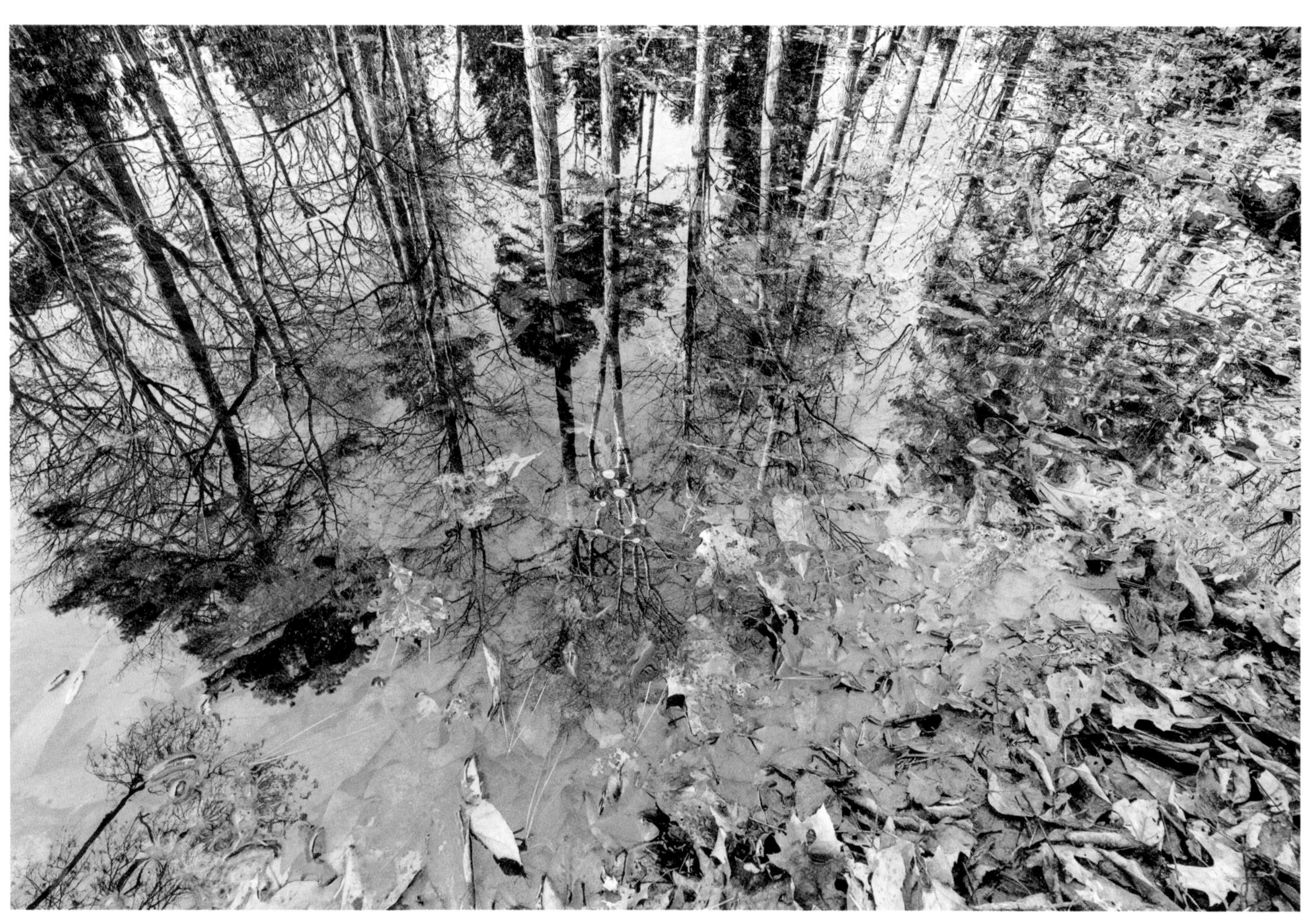

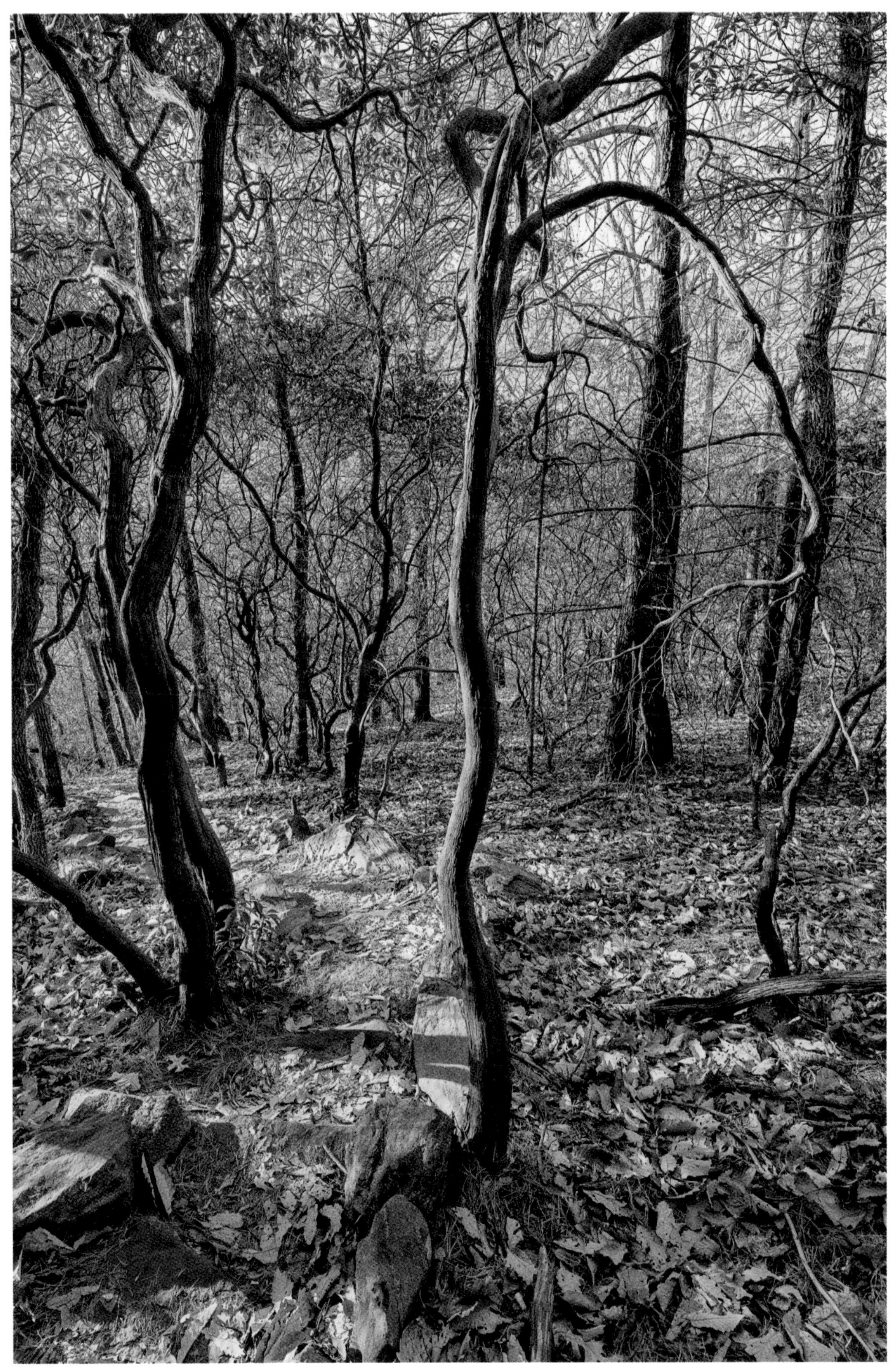

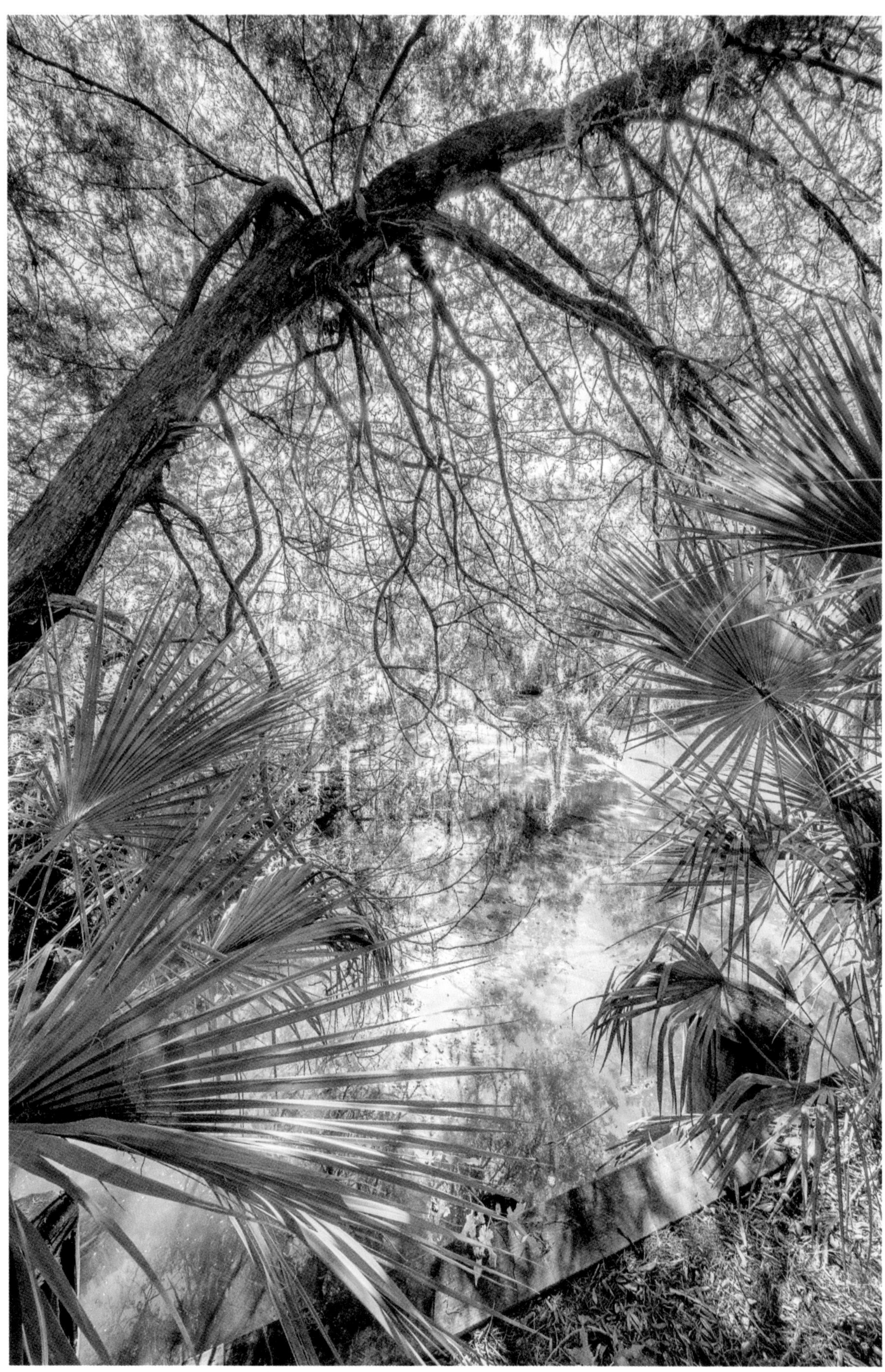

A path through gnarled woods
Branches arch to gather in
Life as it expands

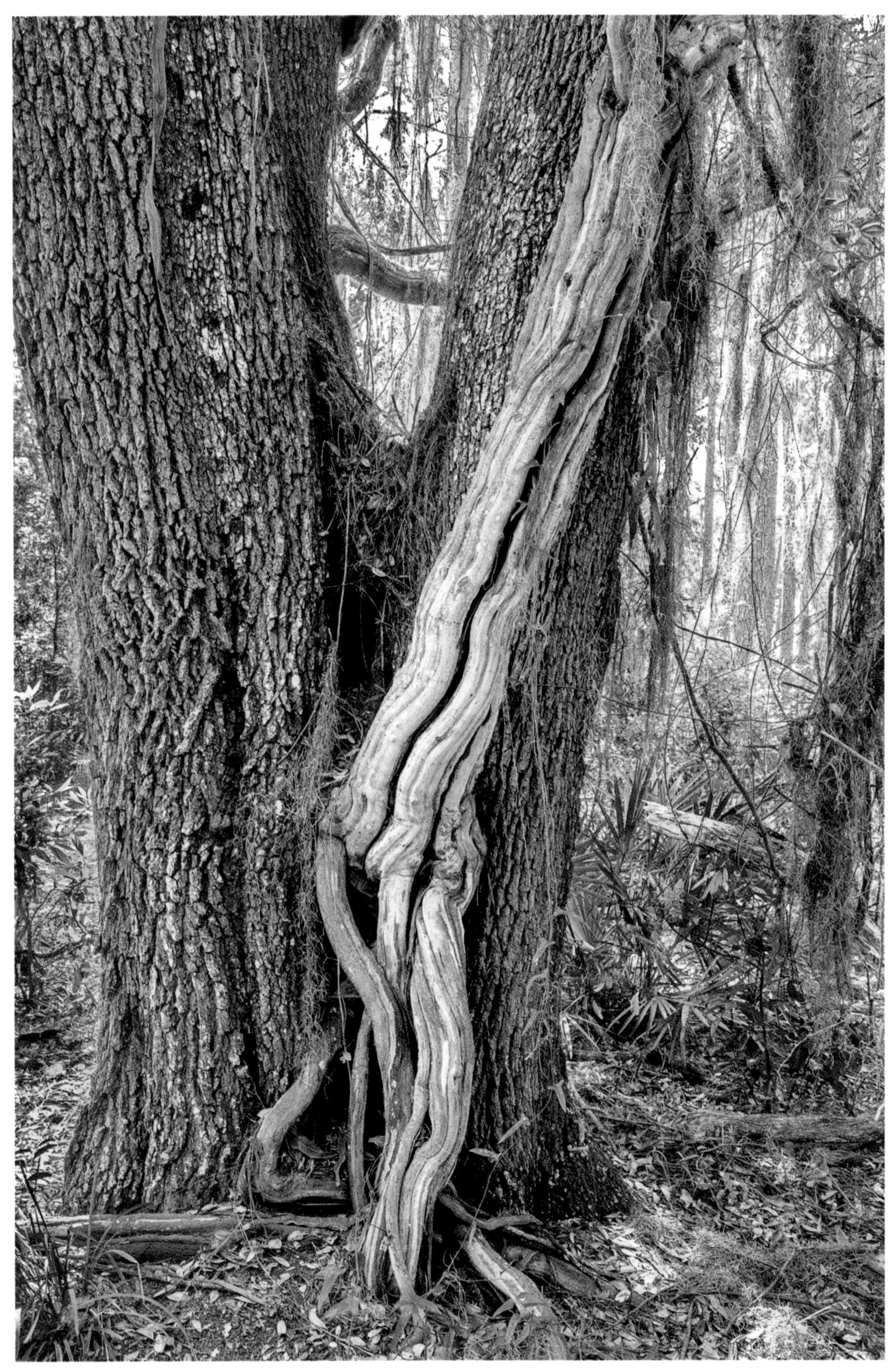

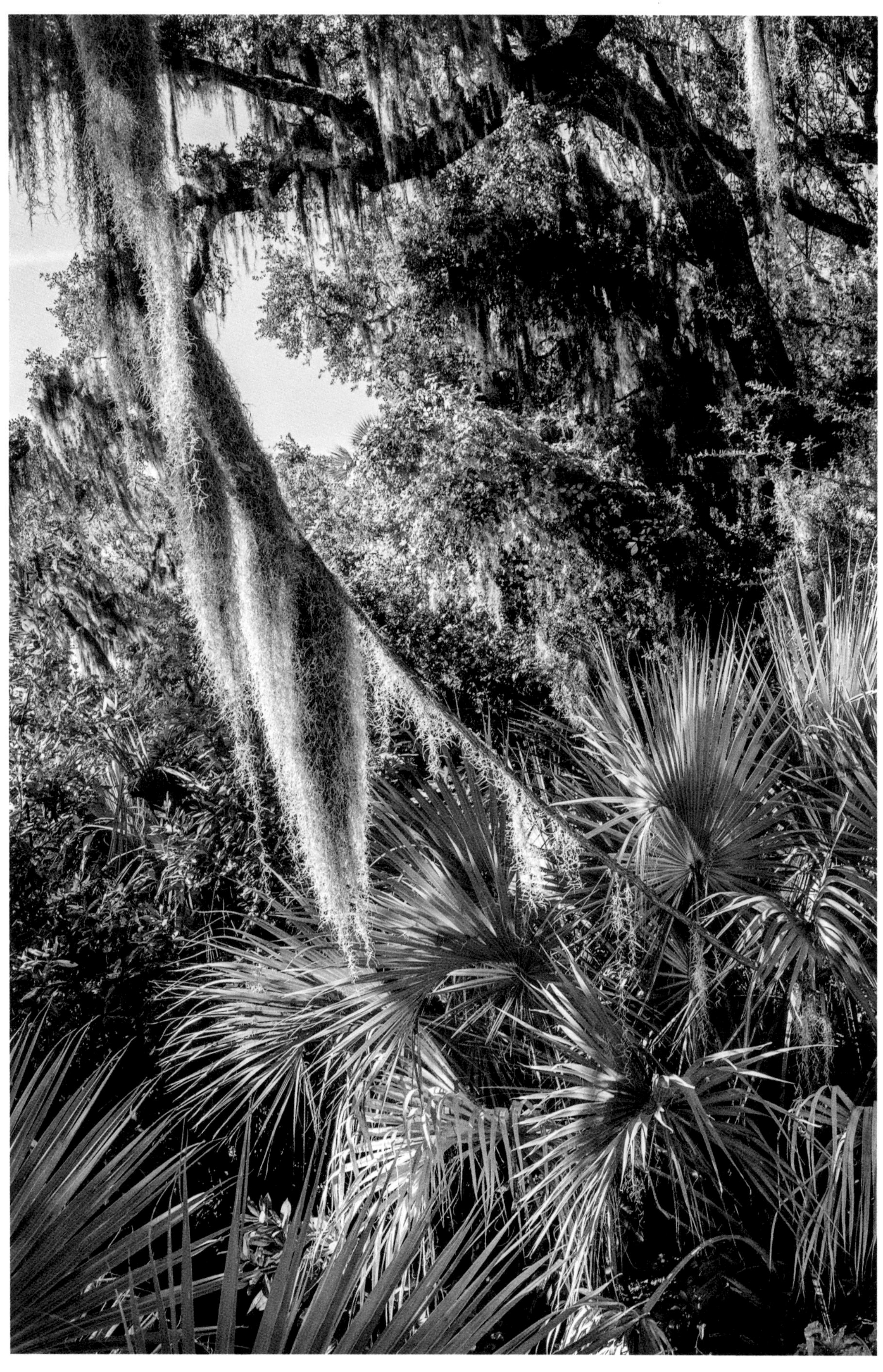

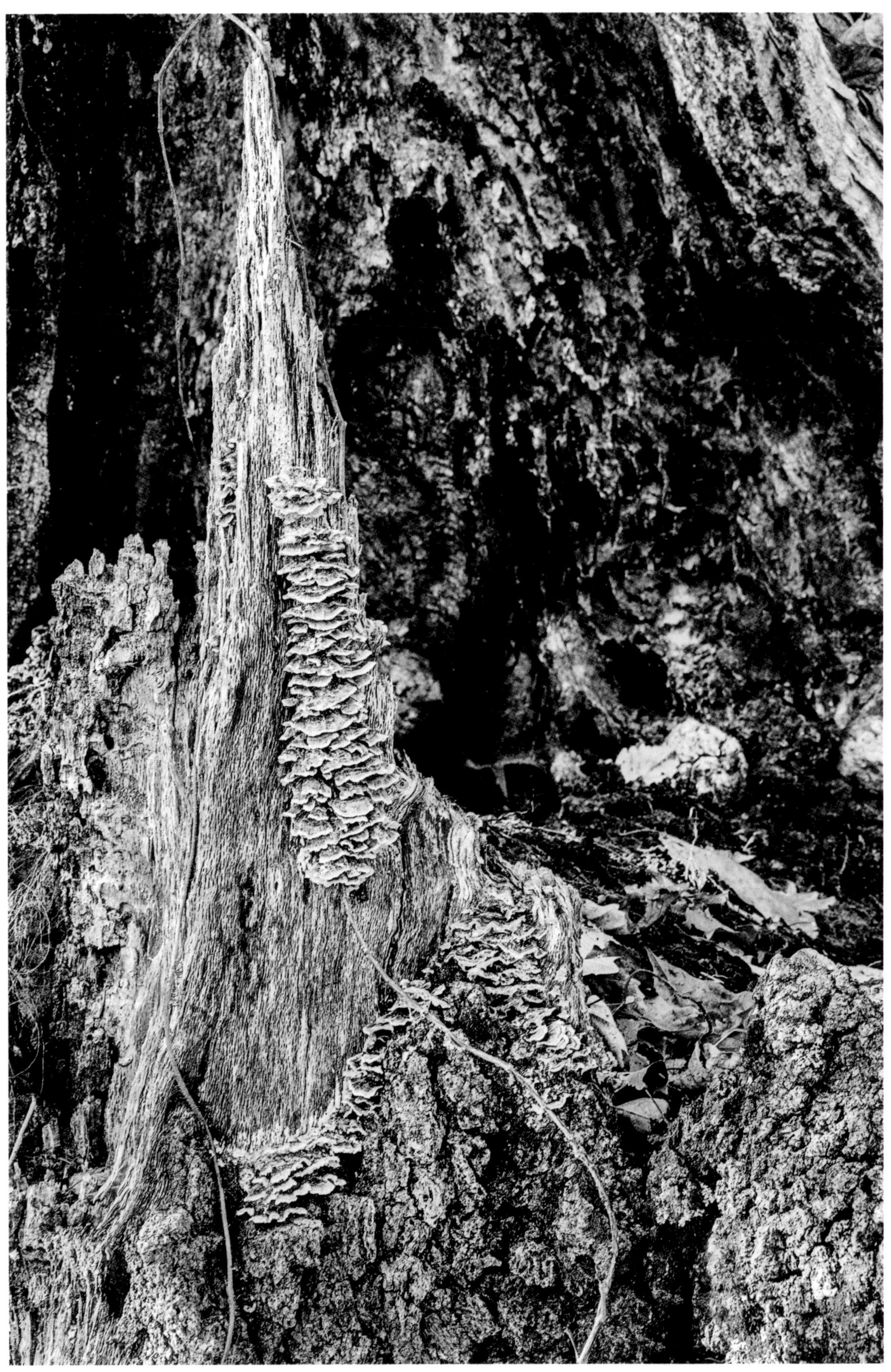

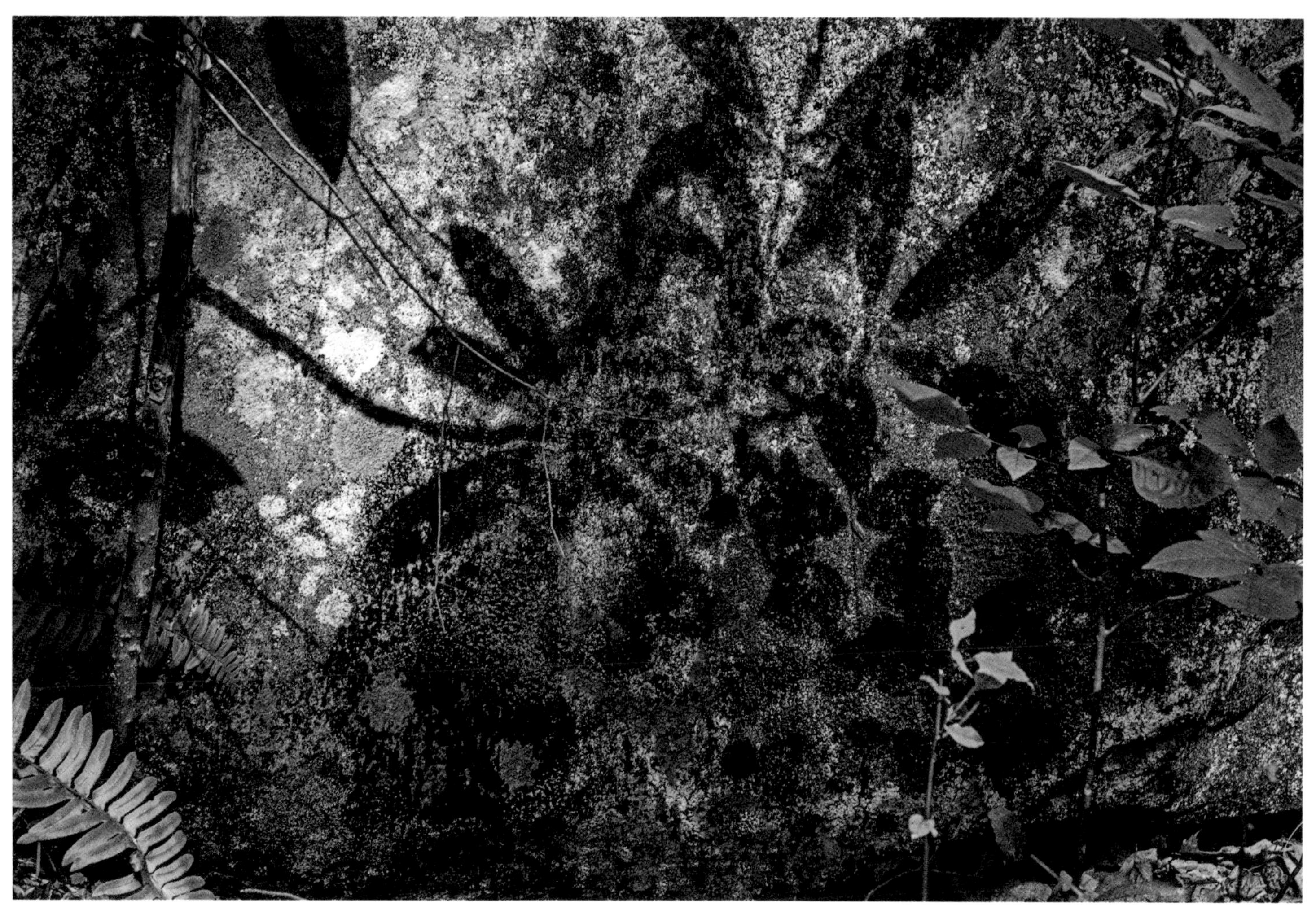

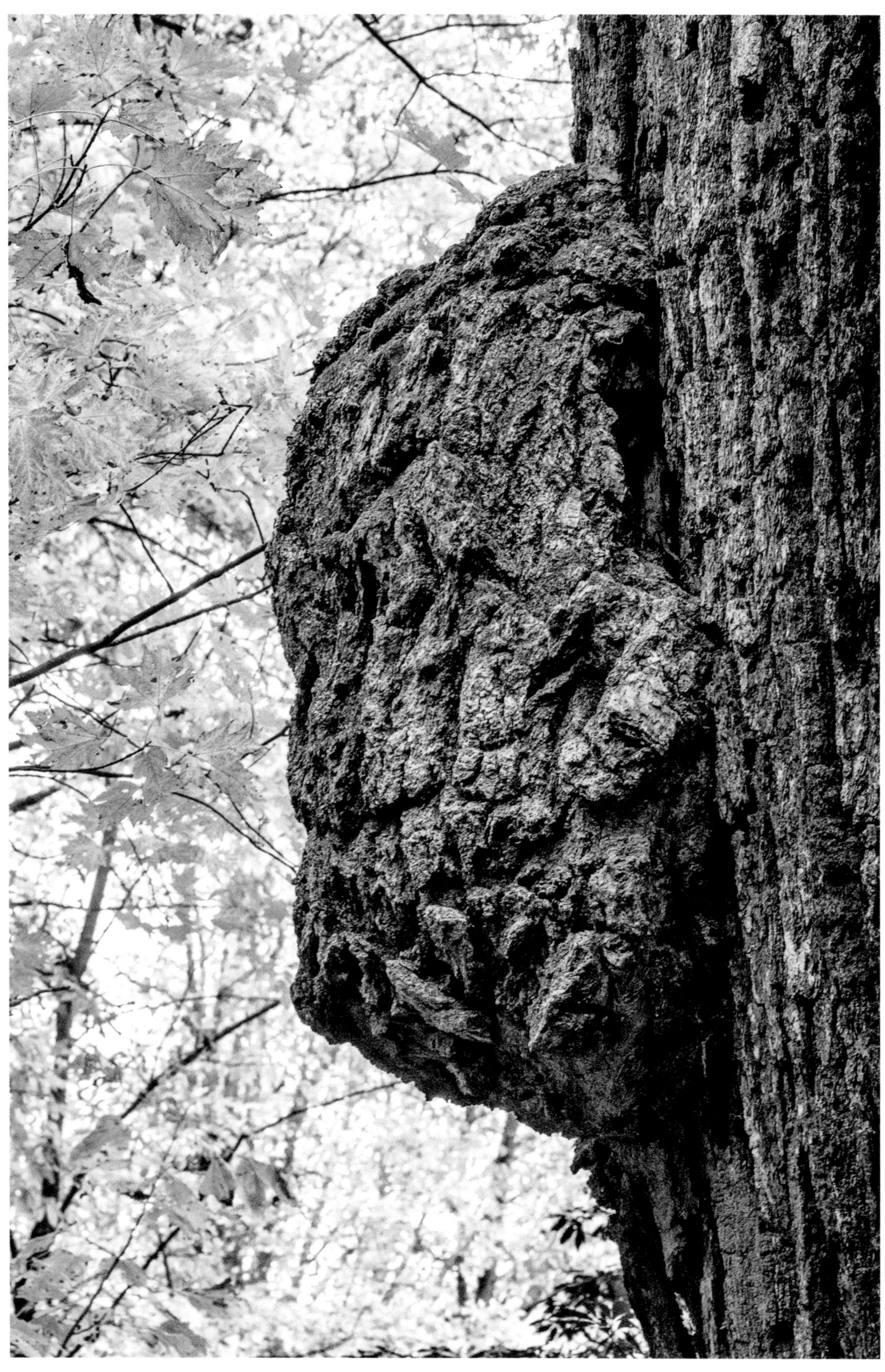

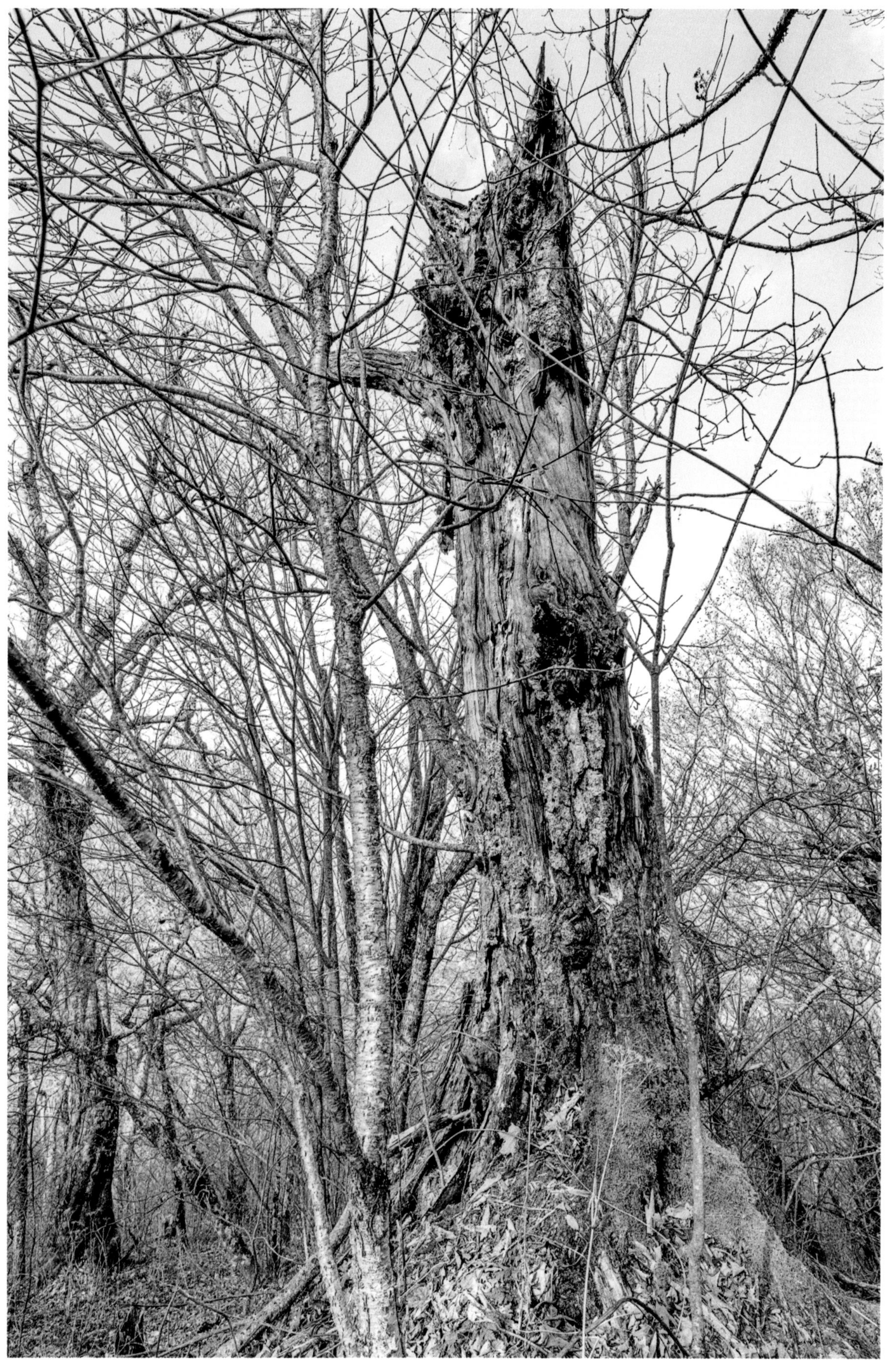

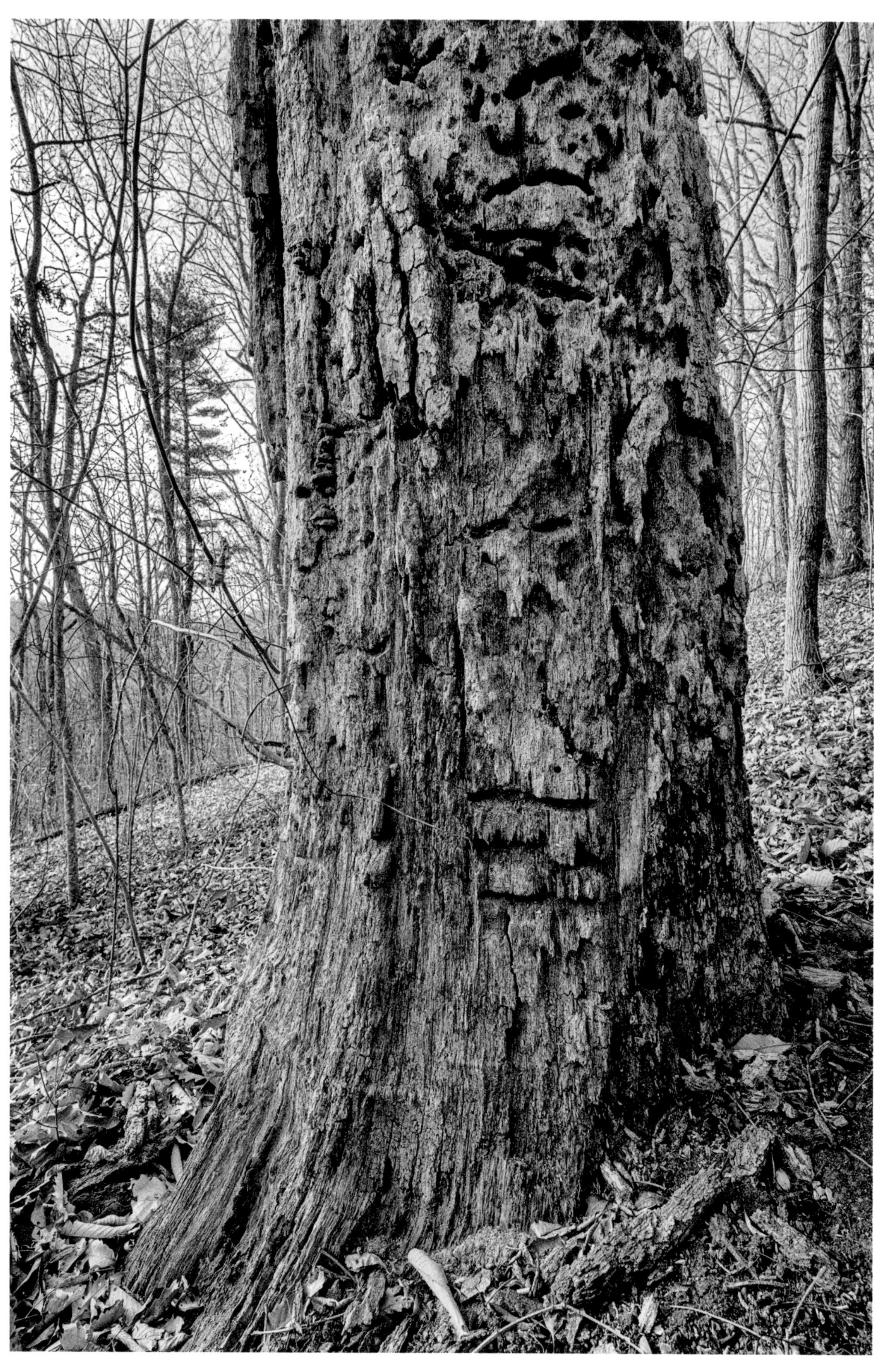

A heart-shaped portal
Hidden in a wall of stone
The future beckons

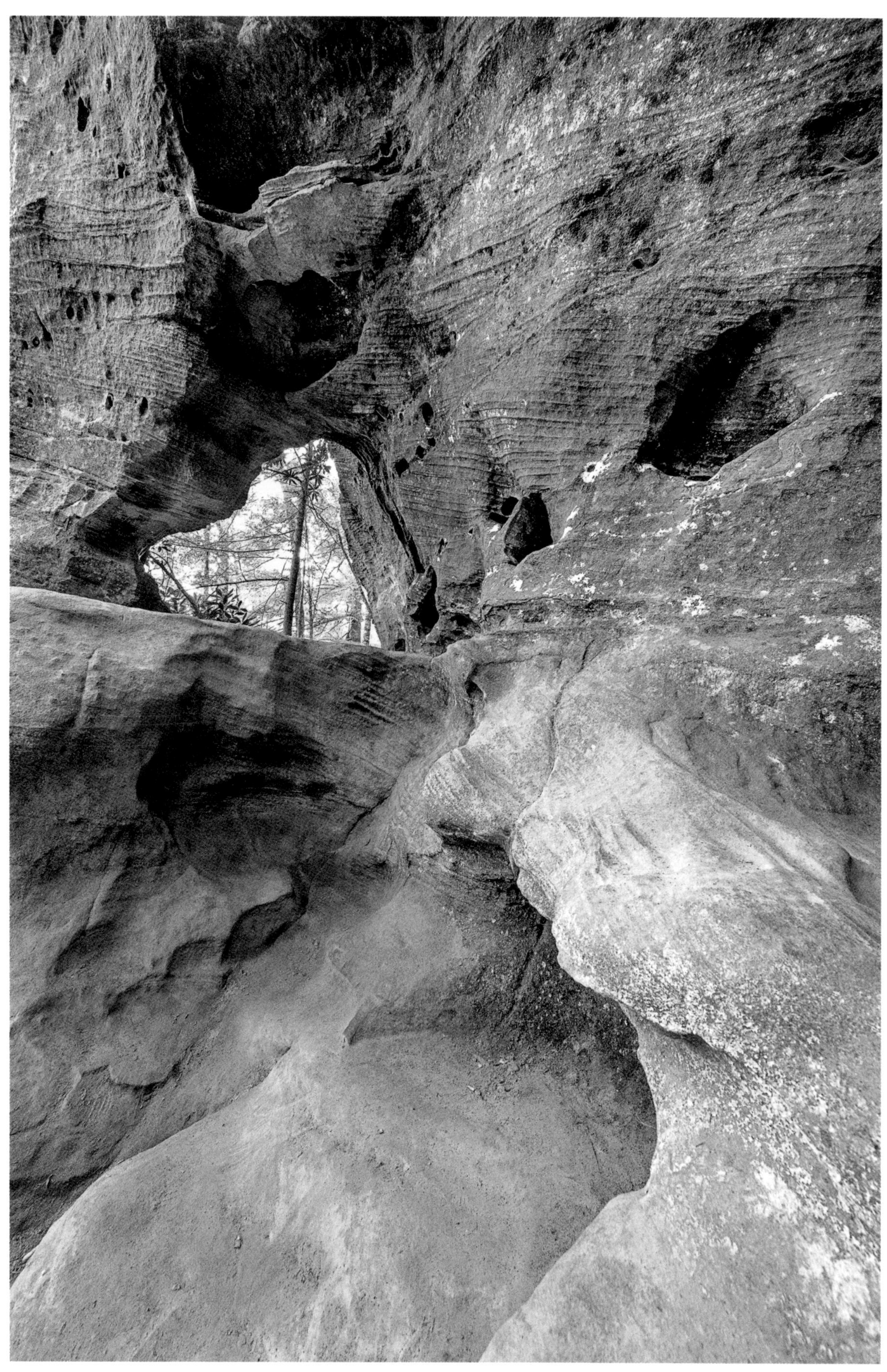

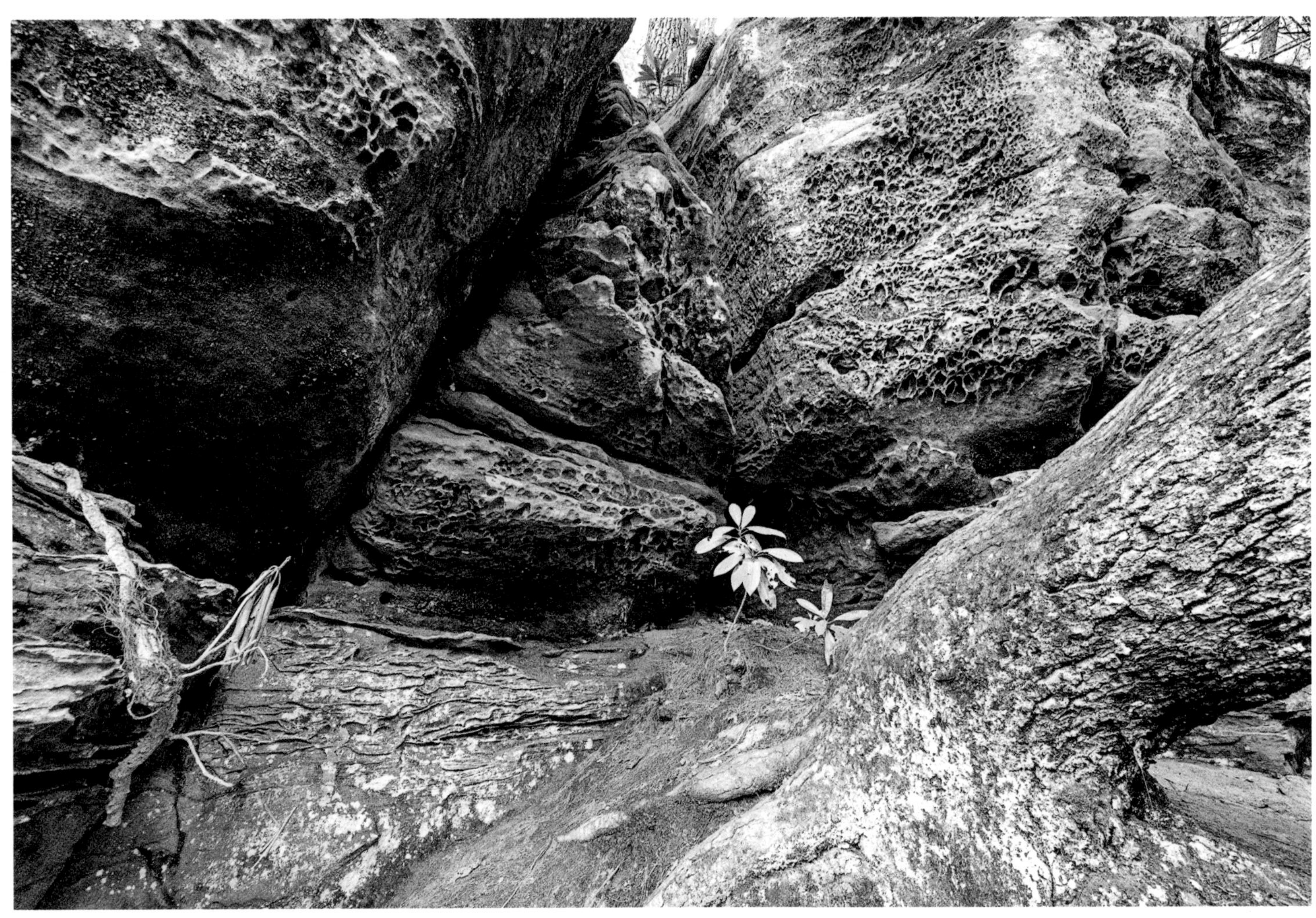

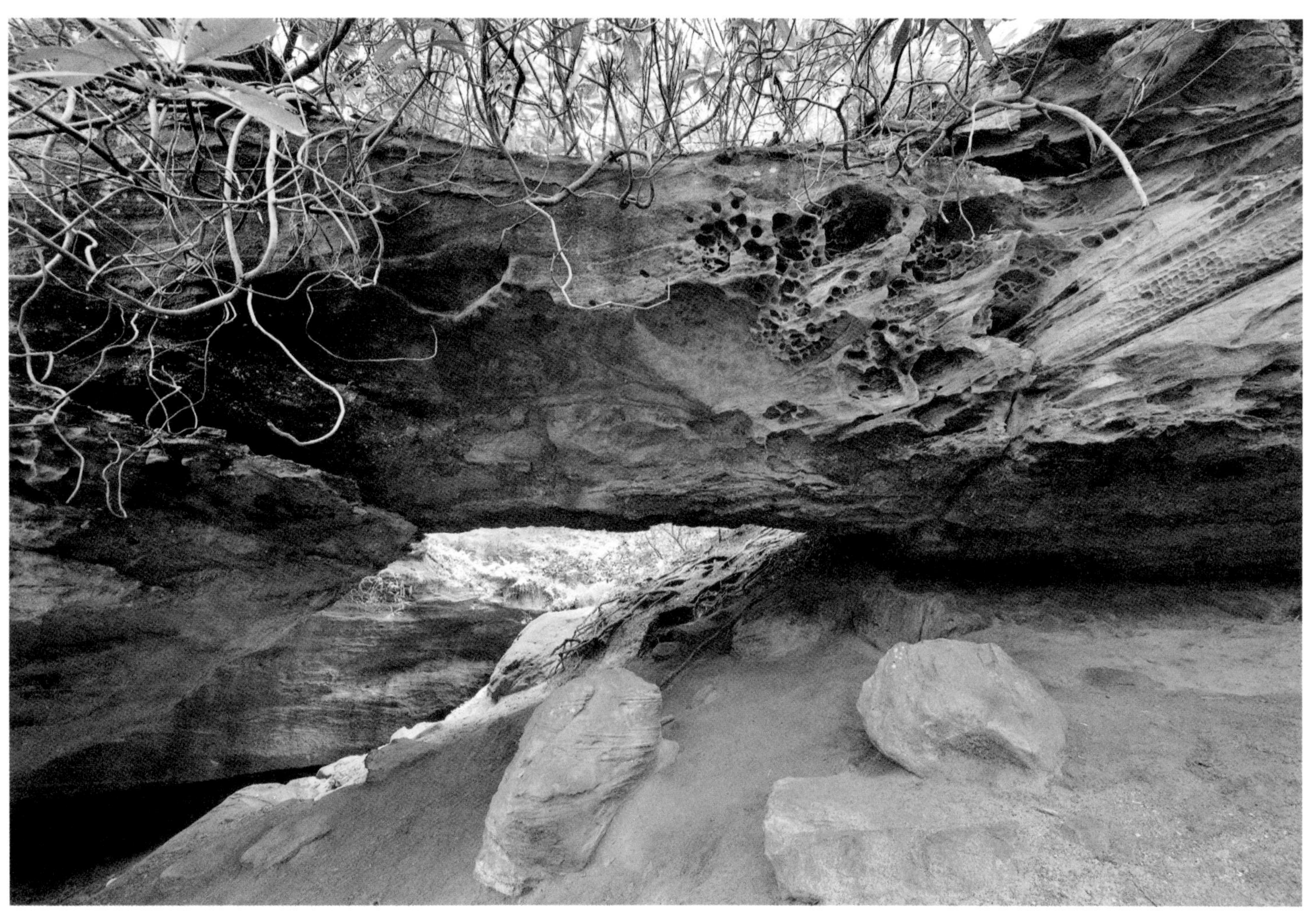

Ancient faces emerge
In a totem carved by insects
History repeats

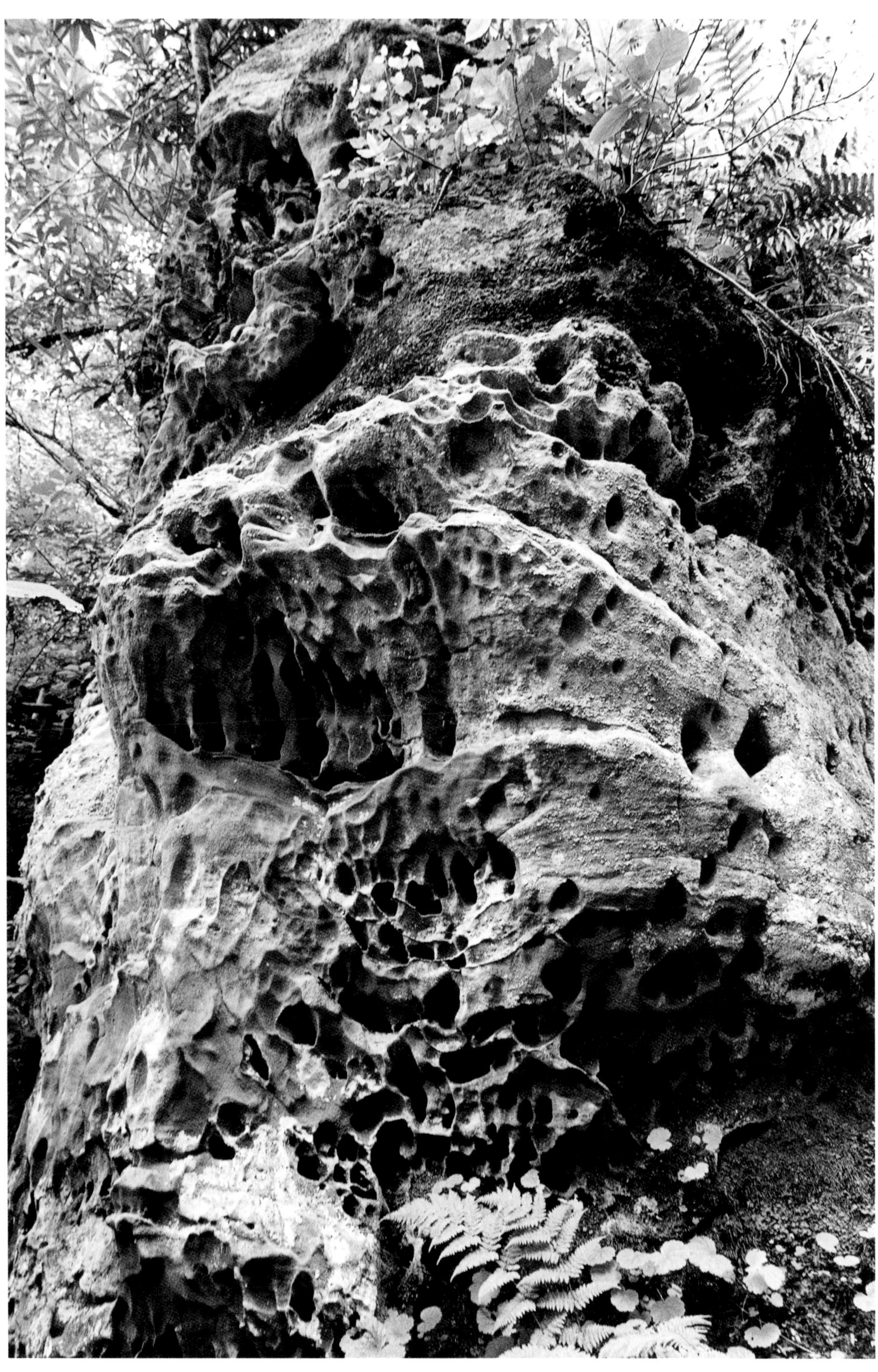

Throughout the seasons
The weight became too great to bear
Still the bark hung on

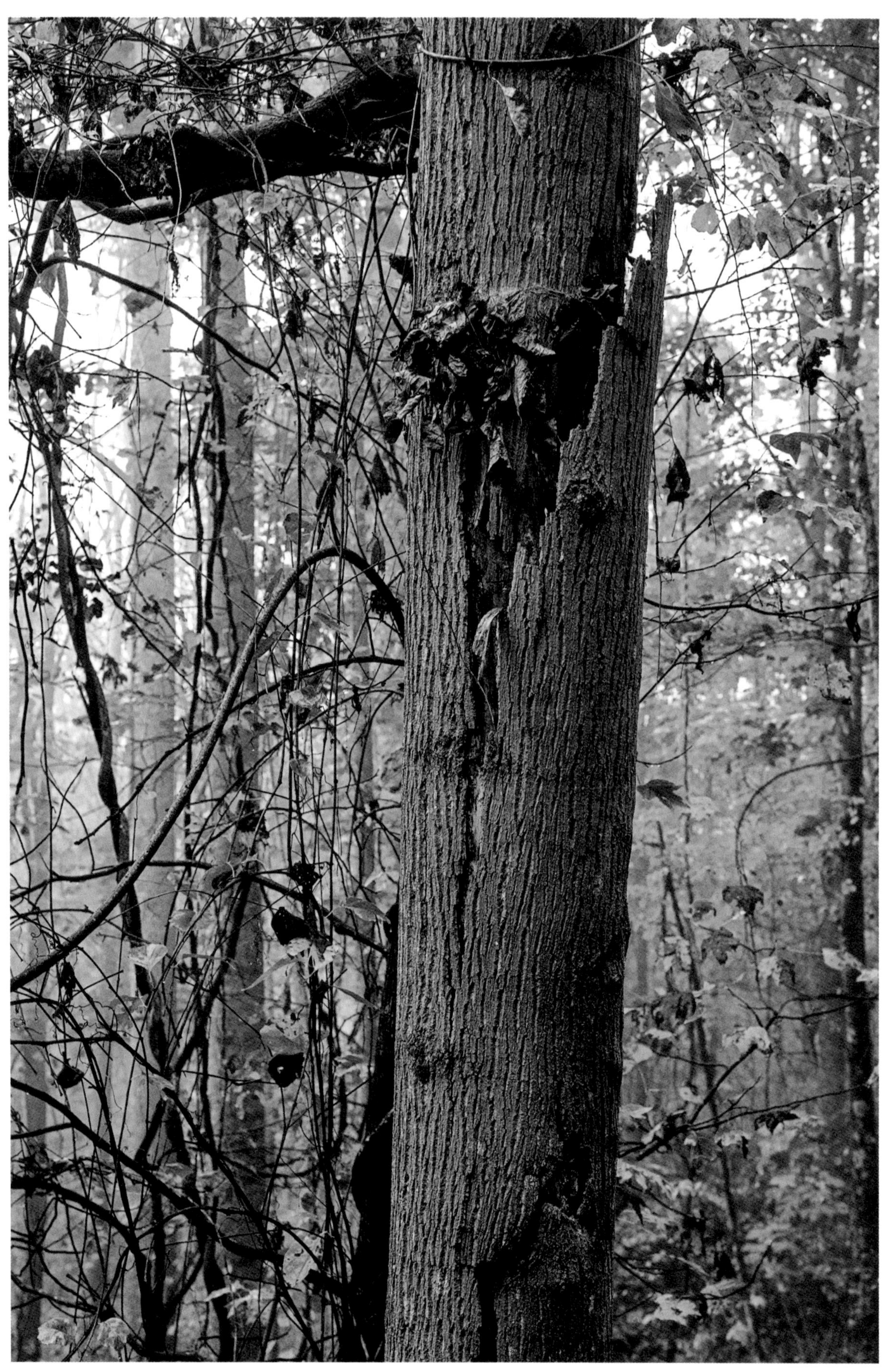

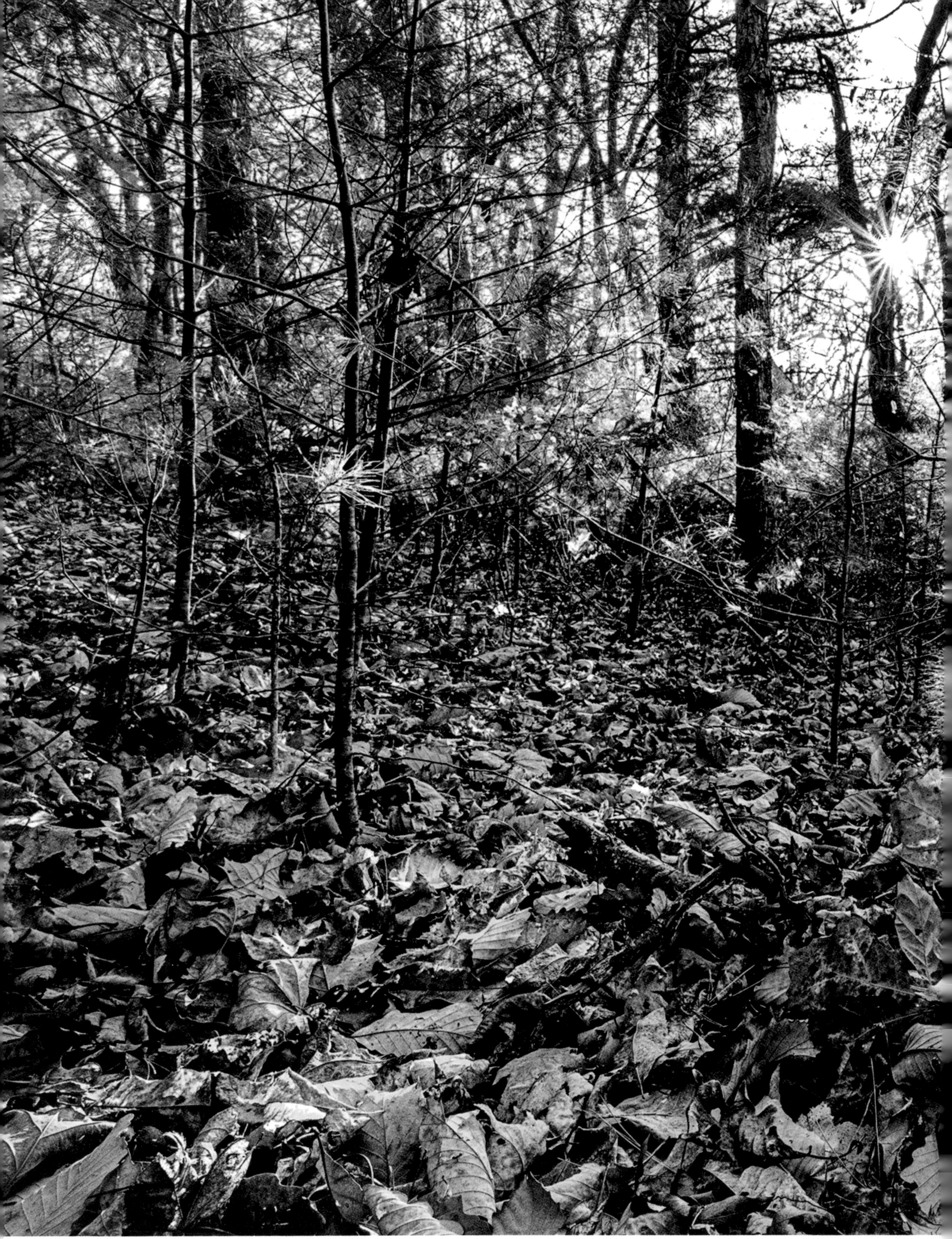

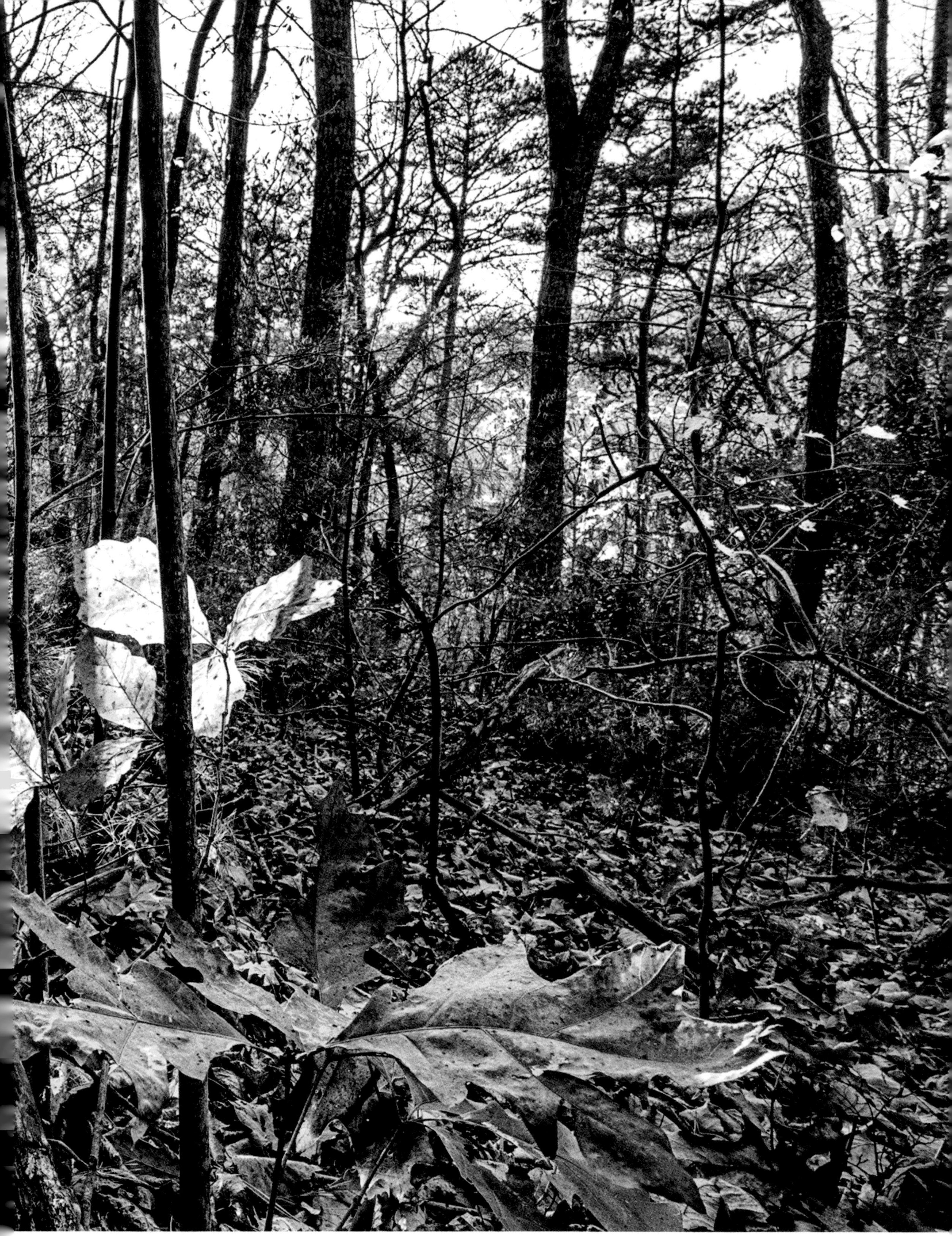

Tangled limbs and logs
The season of falling down
Will soon turn to winter

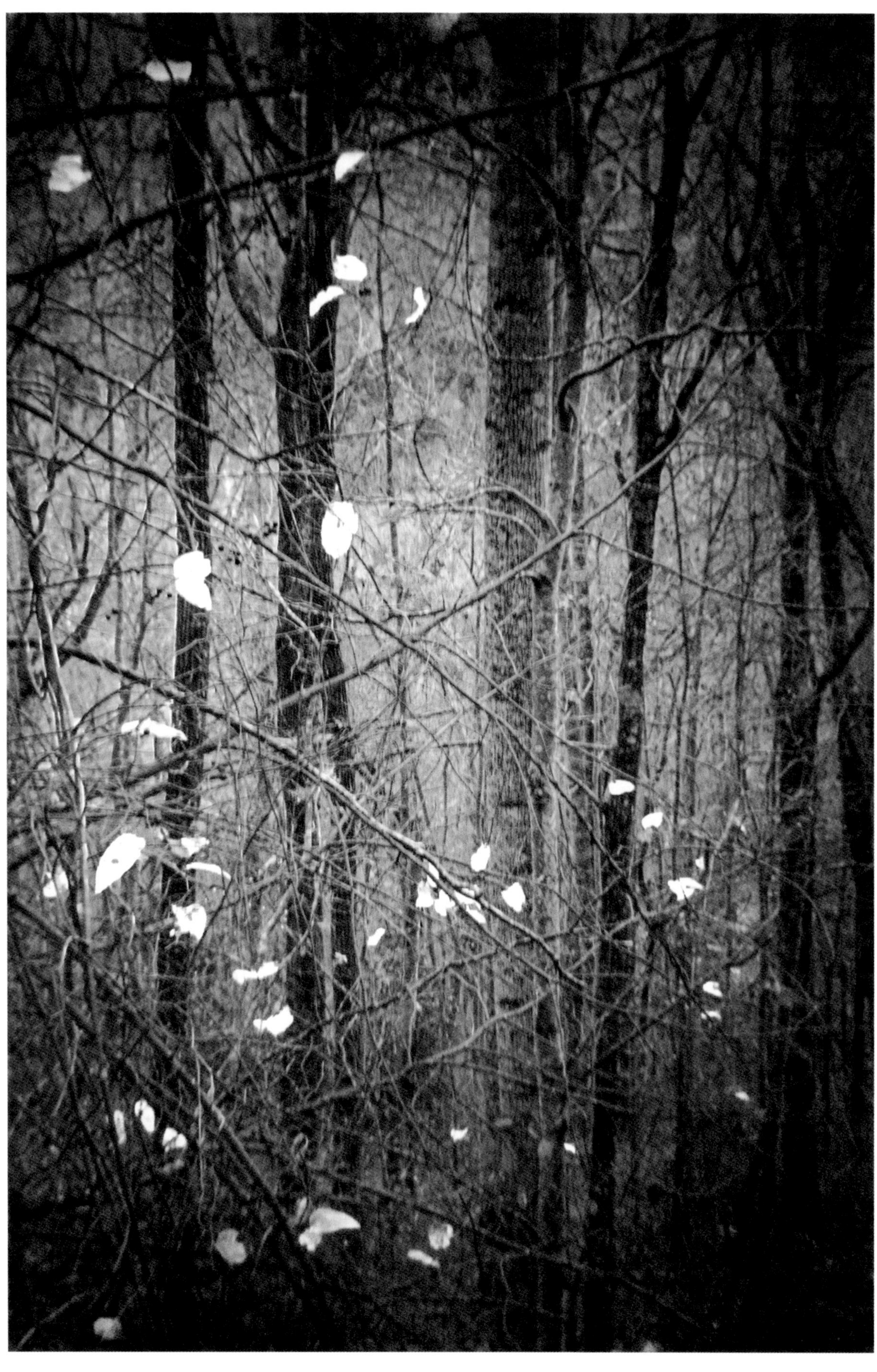

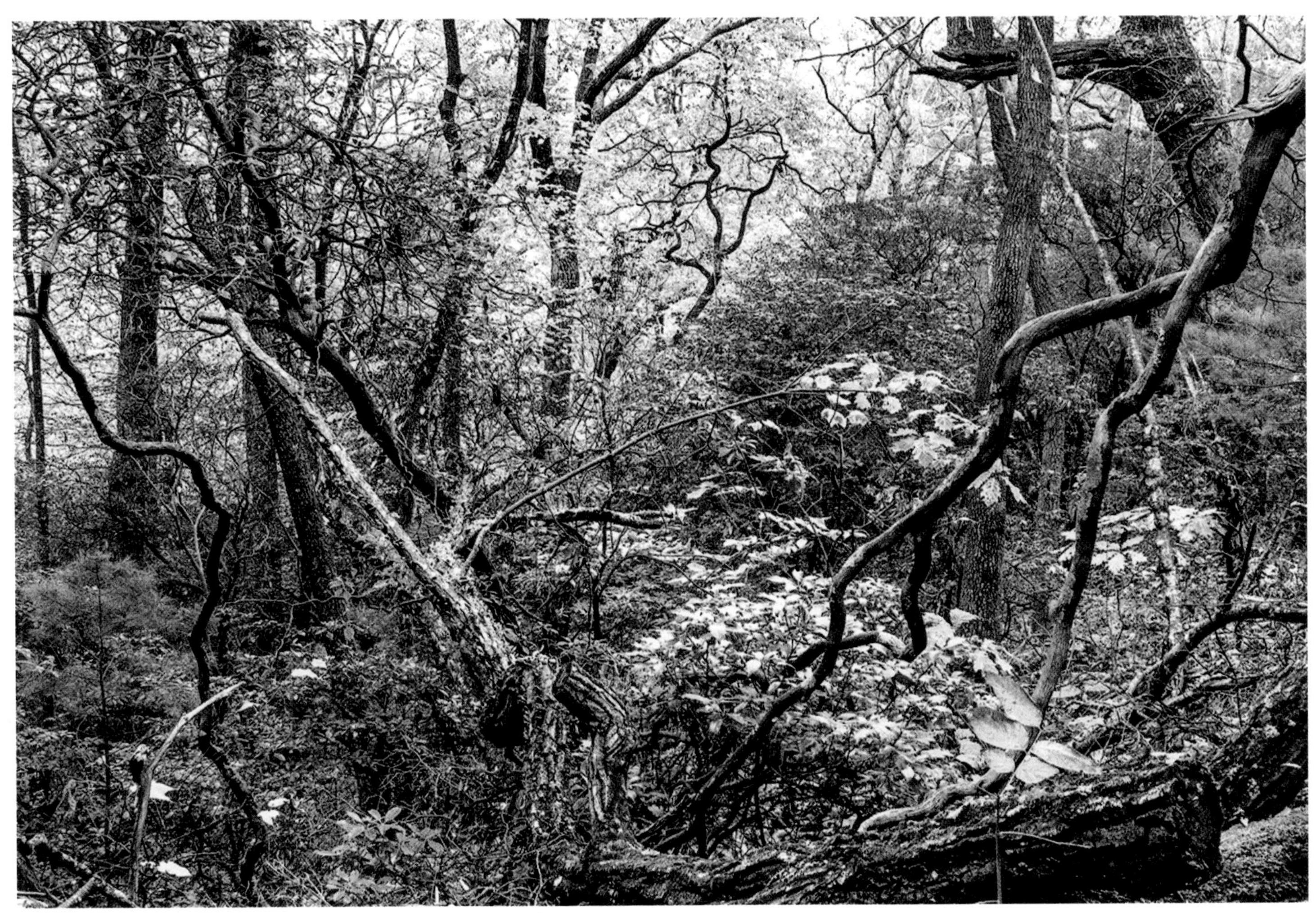

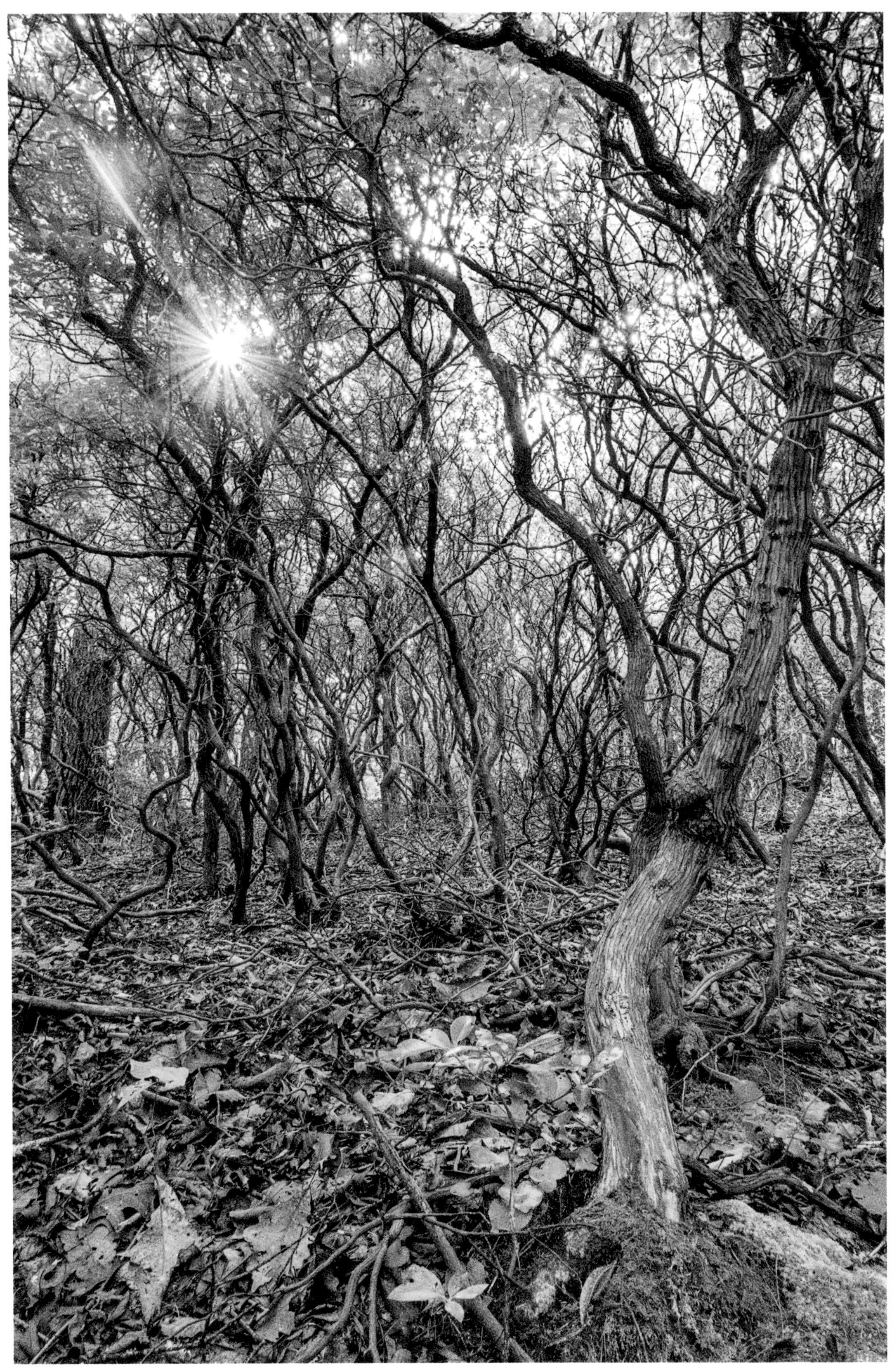

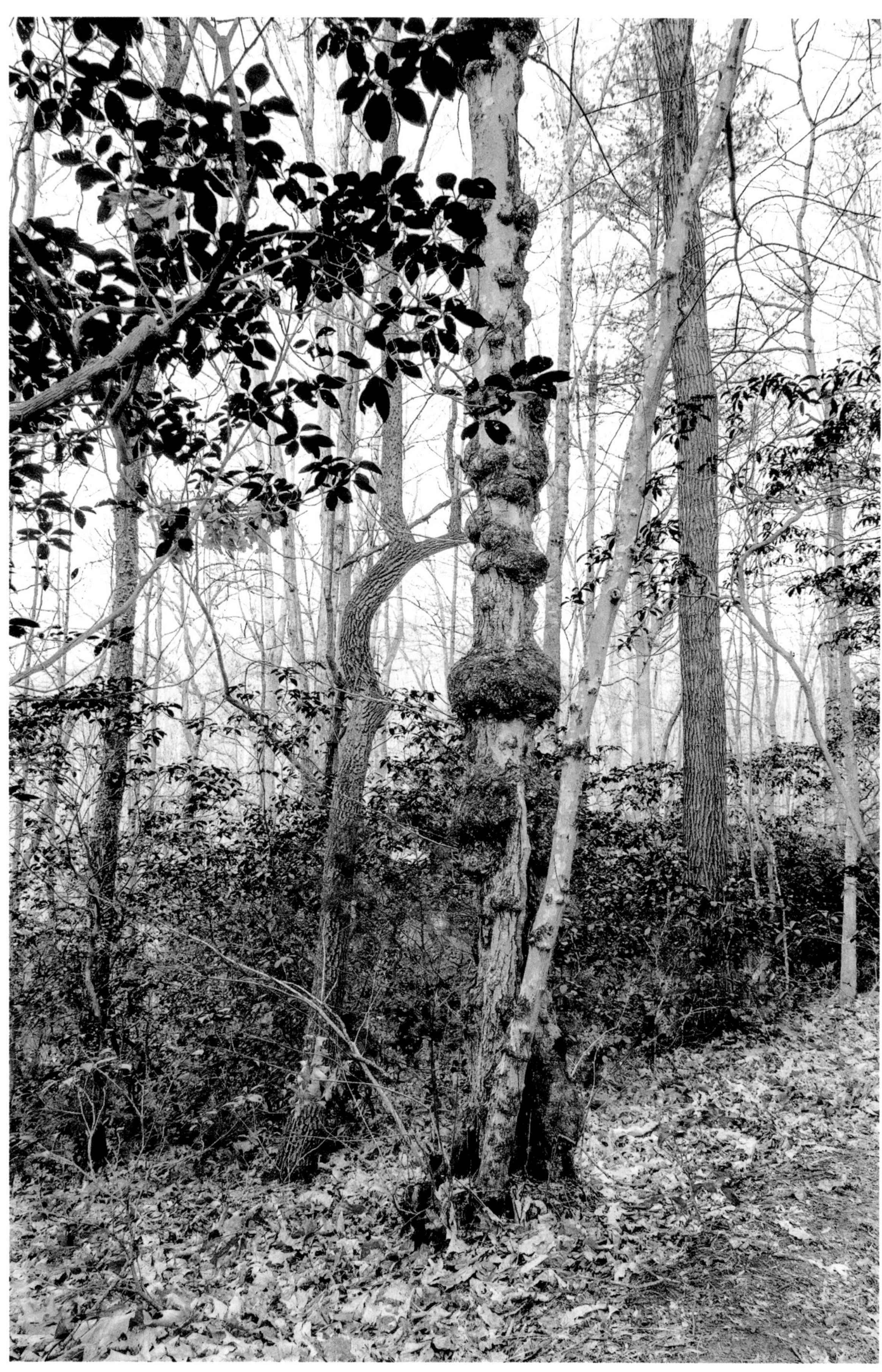

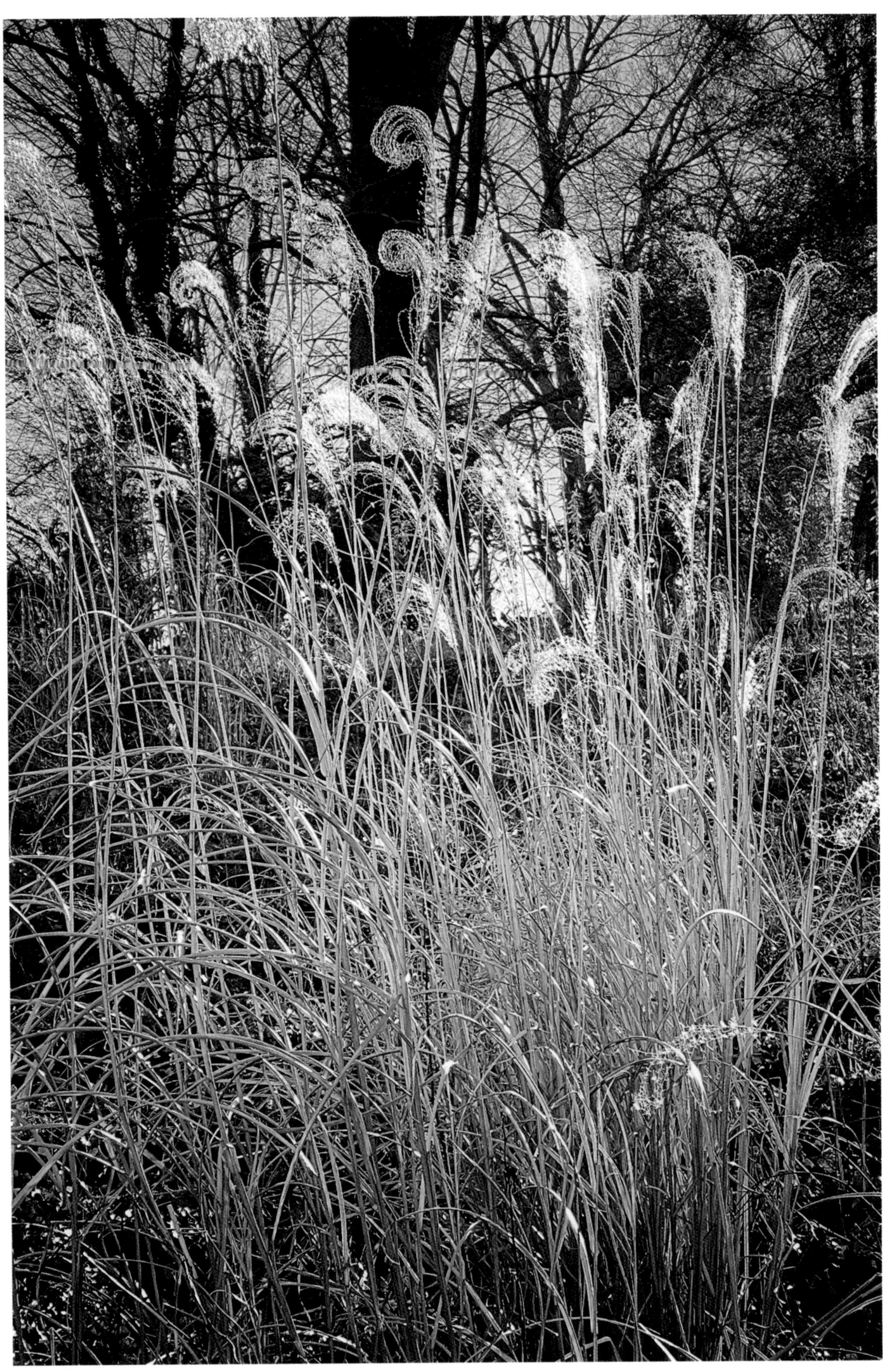

A crack of light remains
Quiet envelops the mountains
Until night comes alive

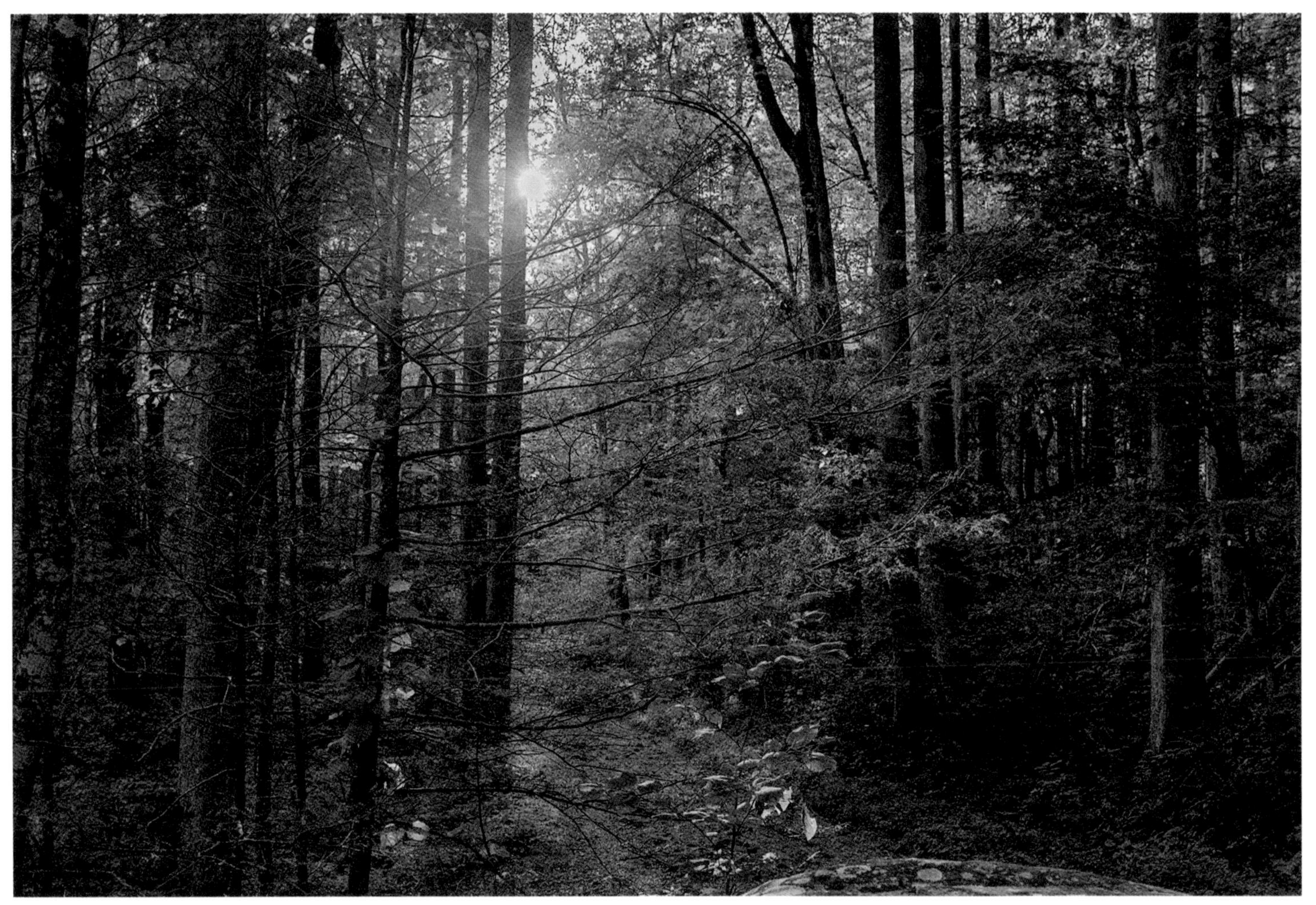

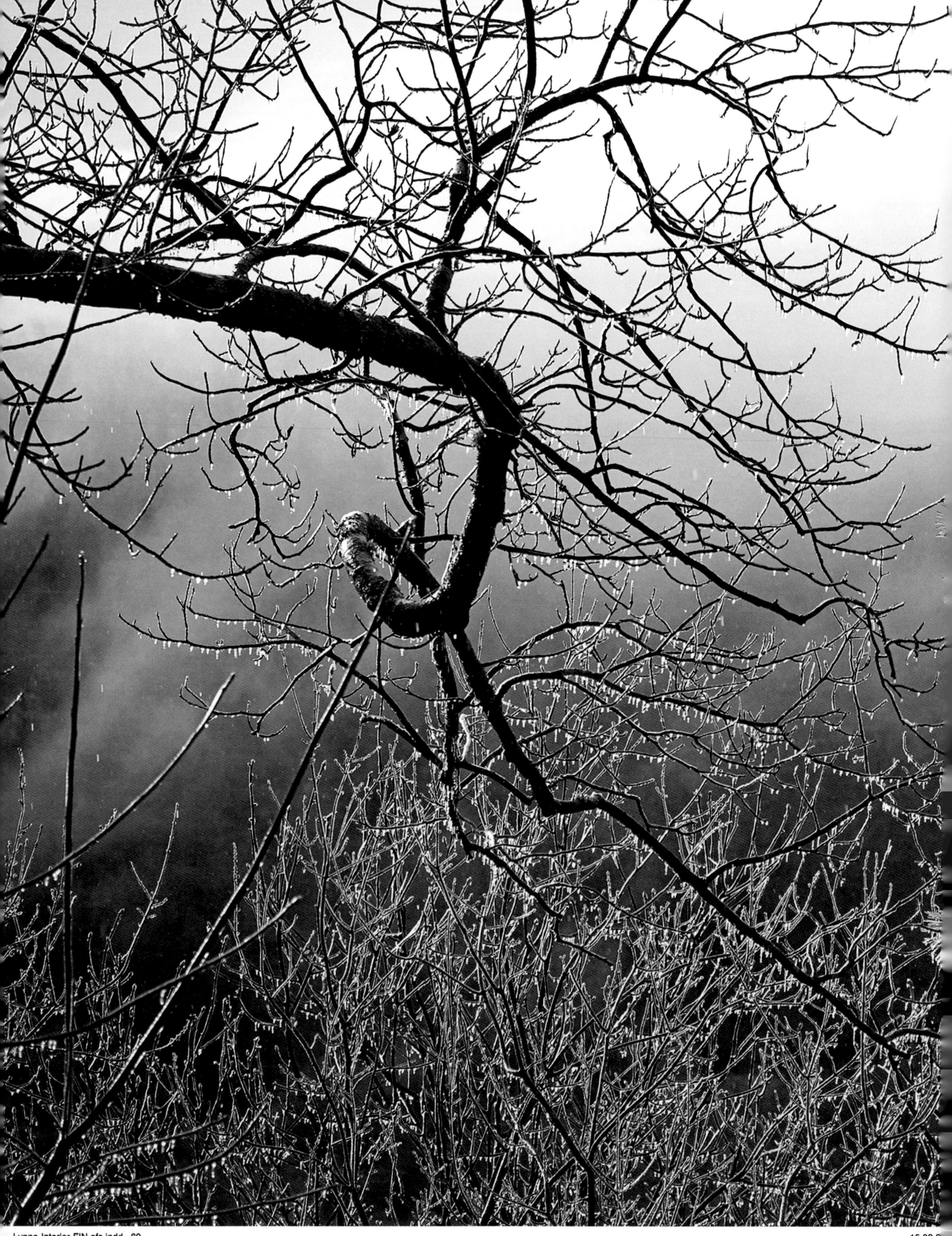

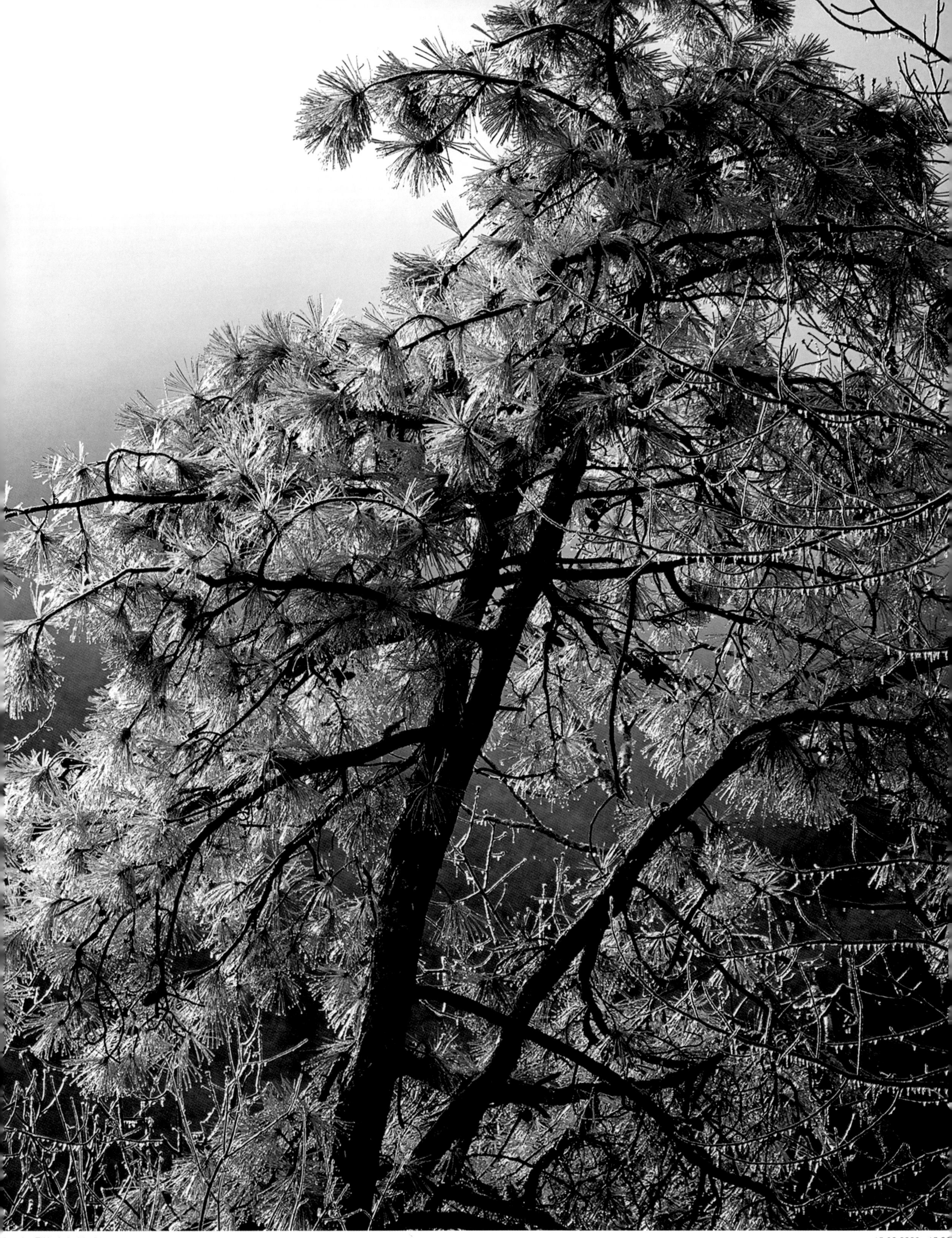

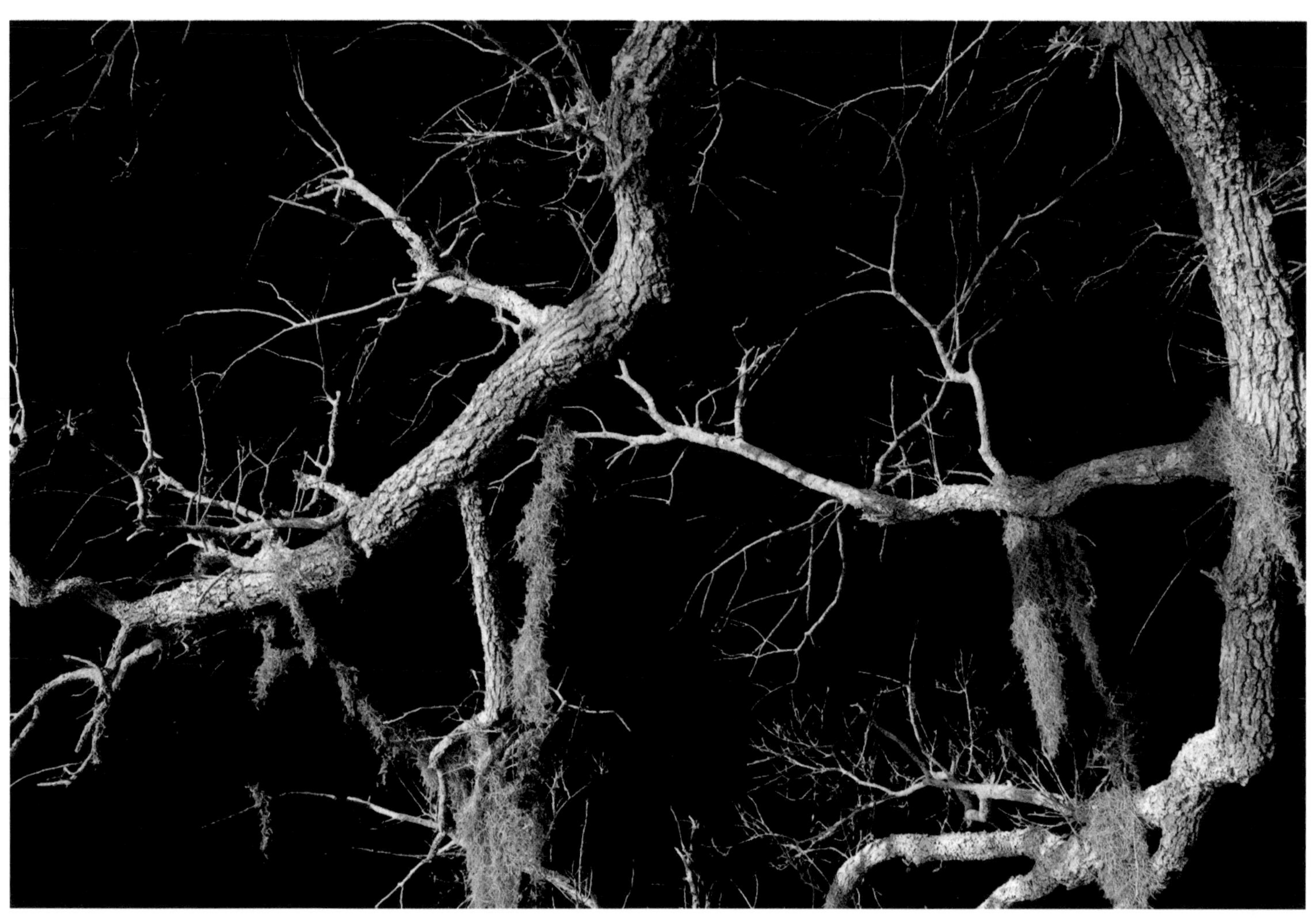

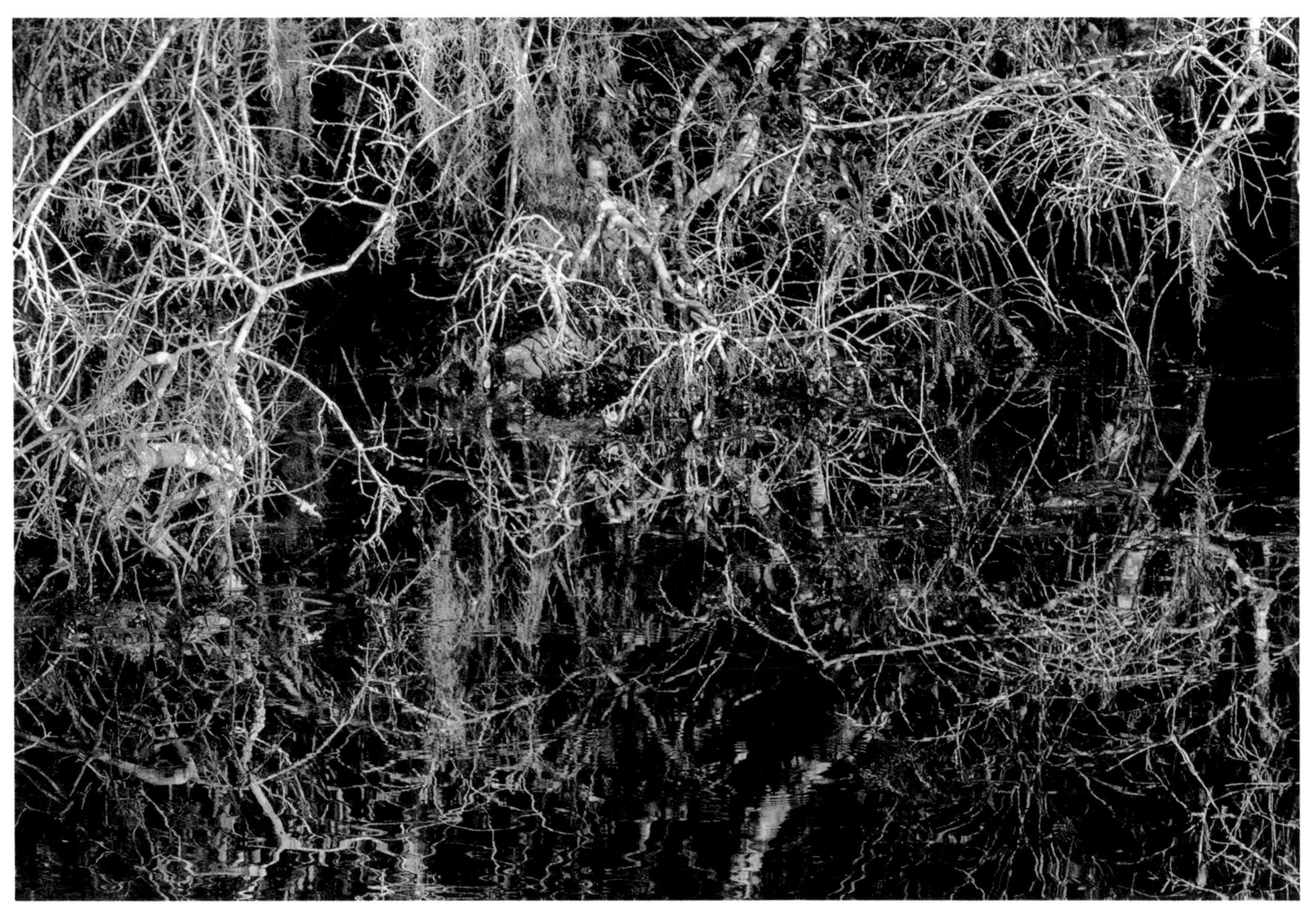

Firm ground is confounded
By exposed roots and bare branches
The earth is shifting

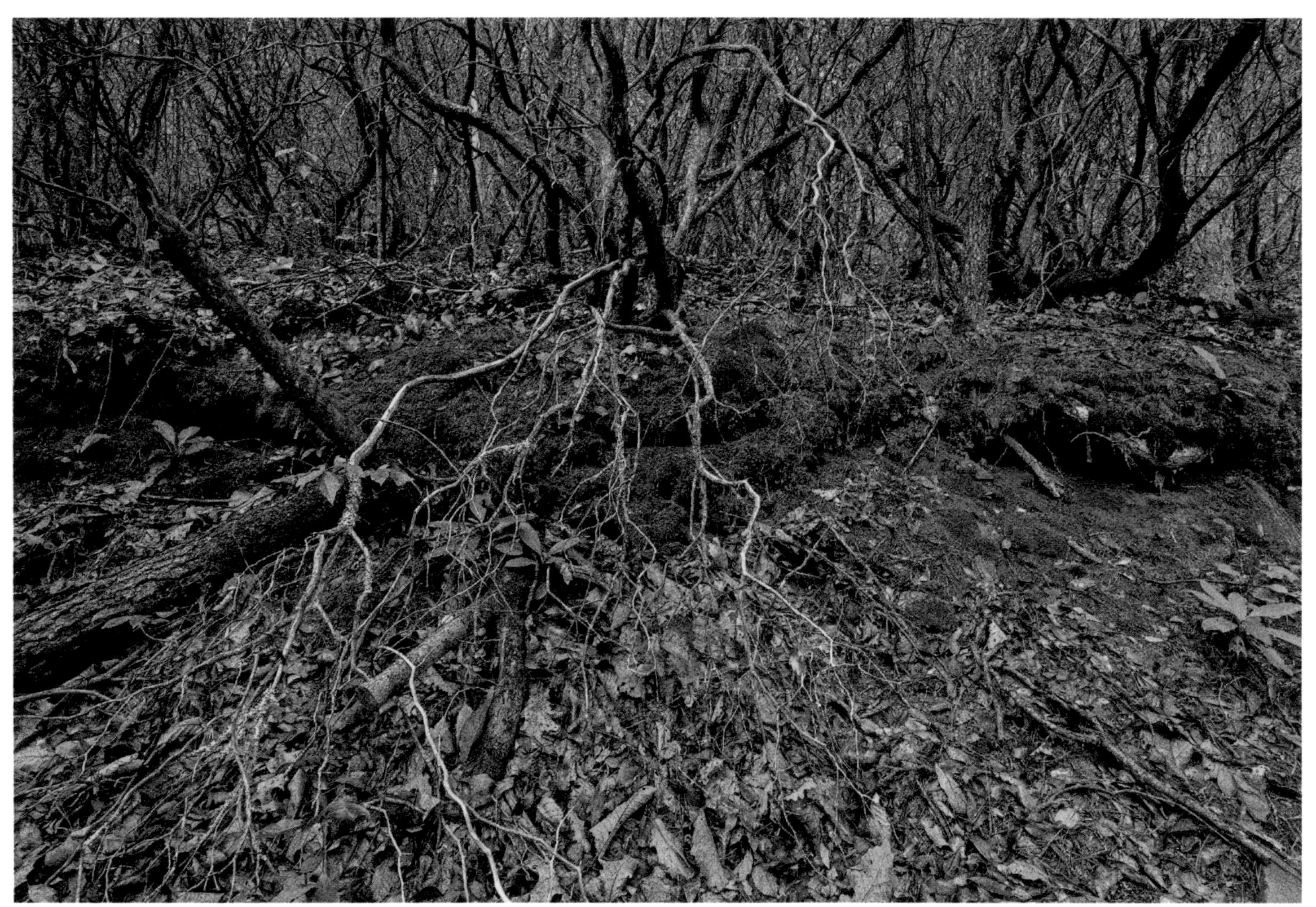

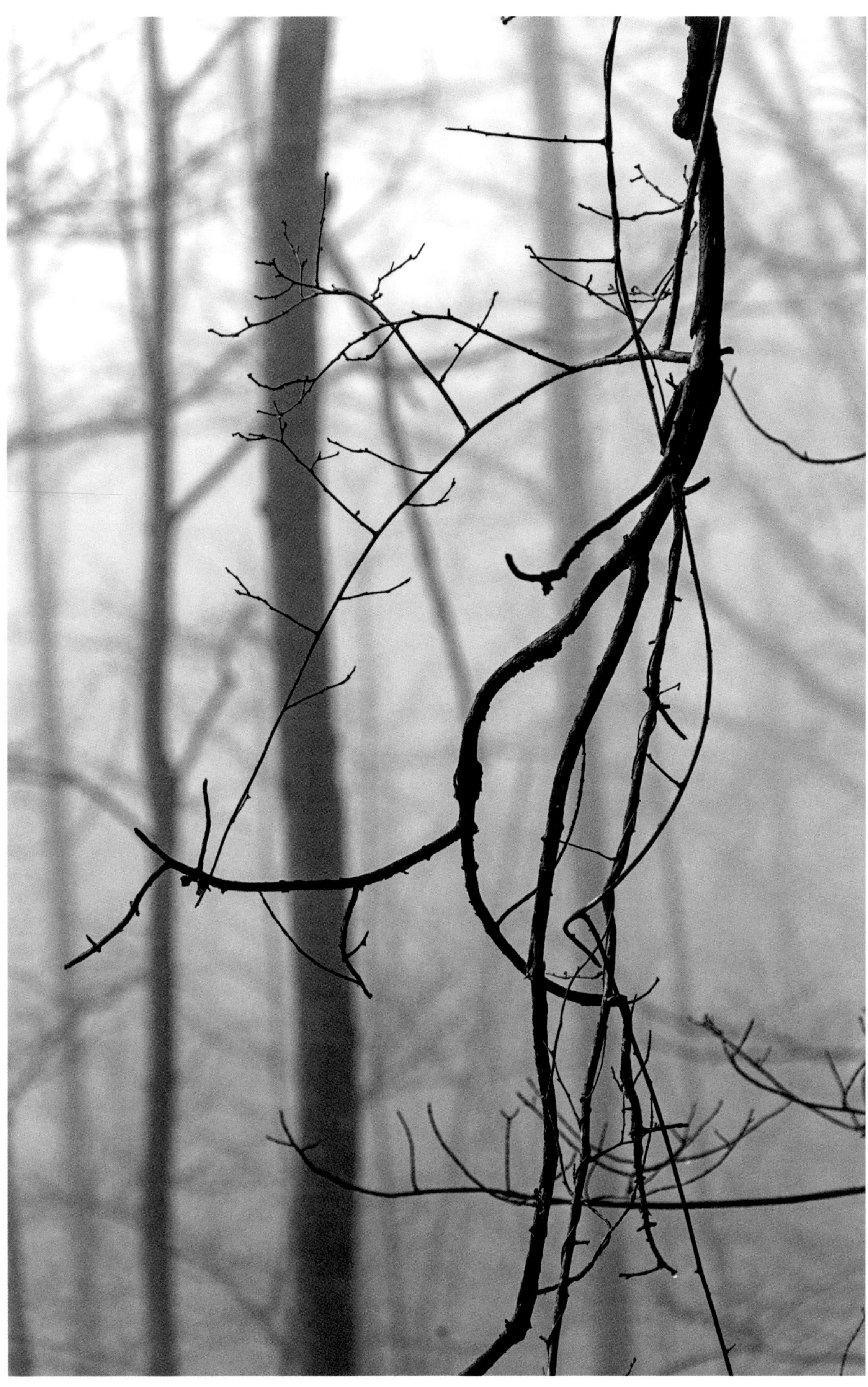

A forest's missive
Written by twigs in winter
Believe seasons change

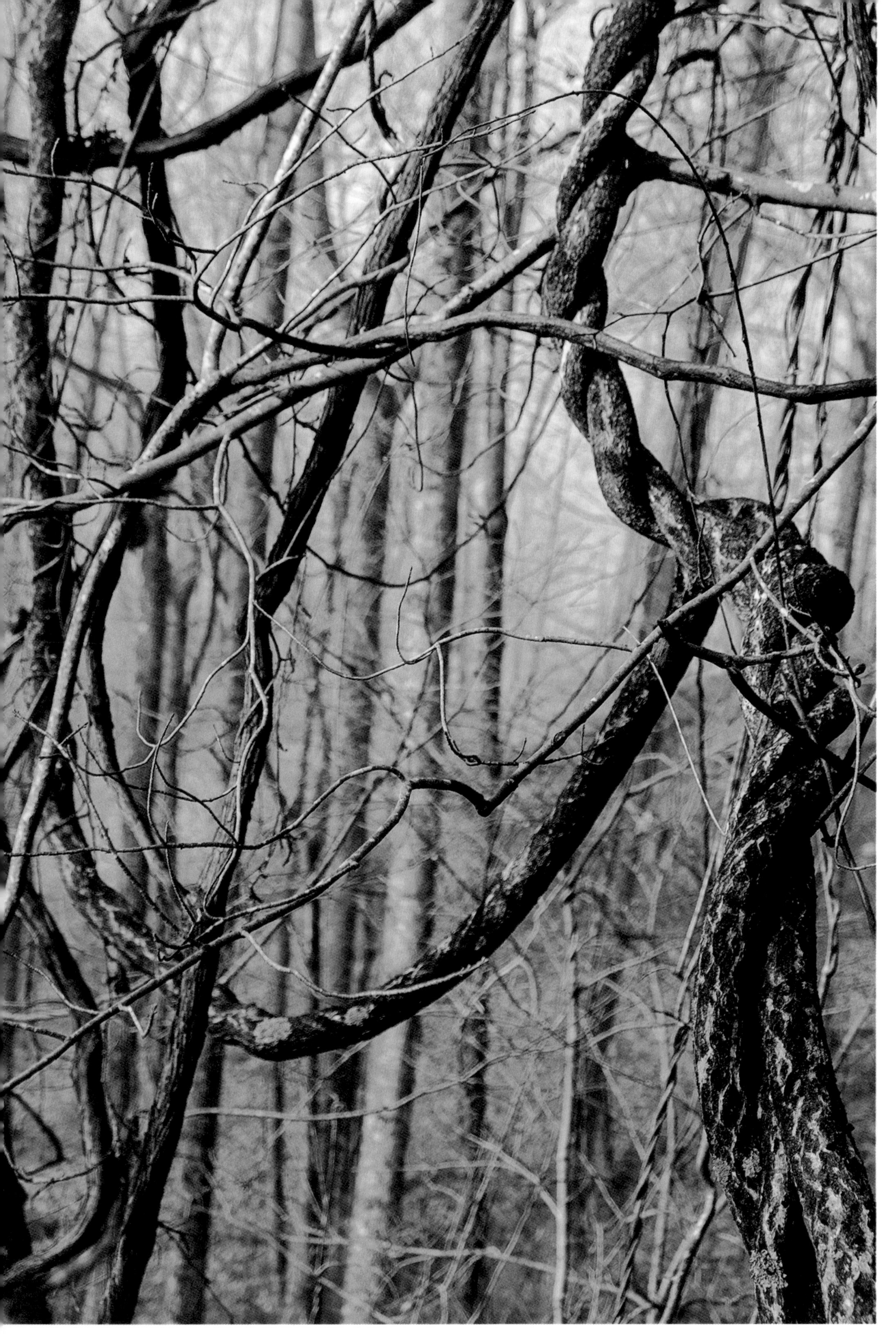

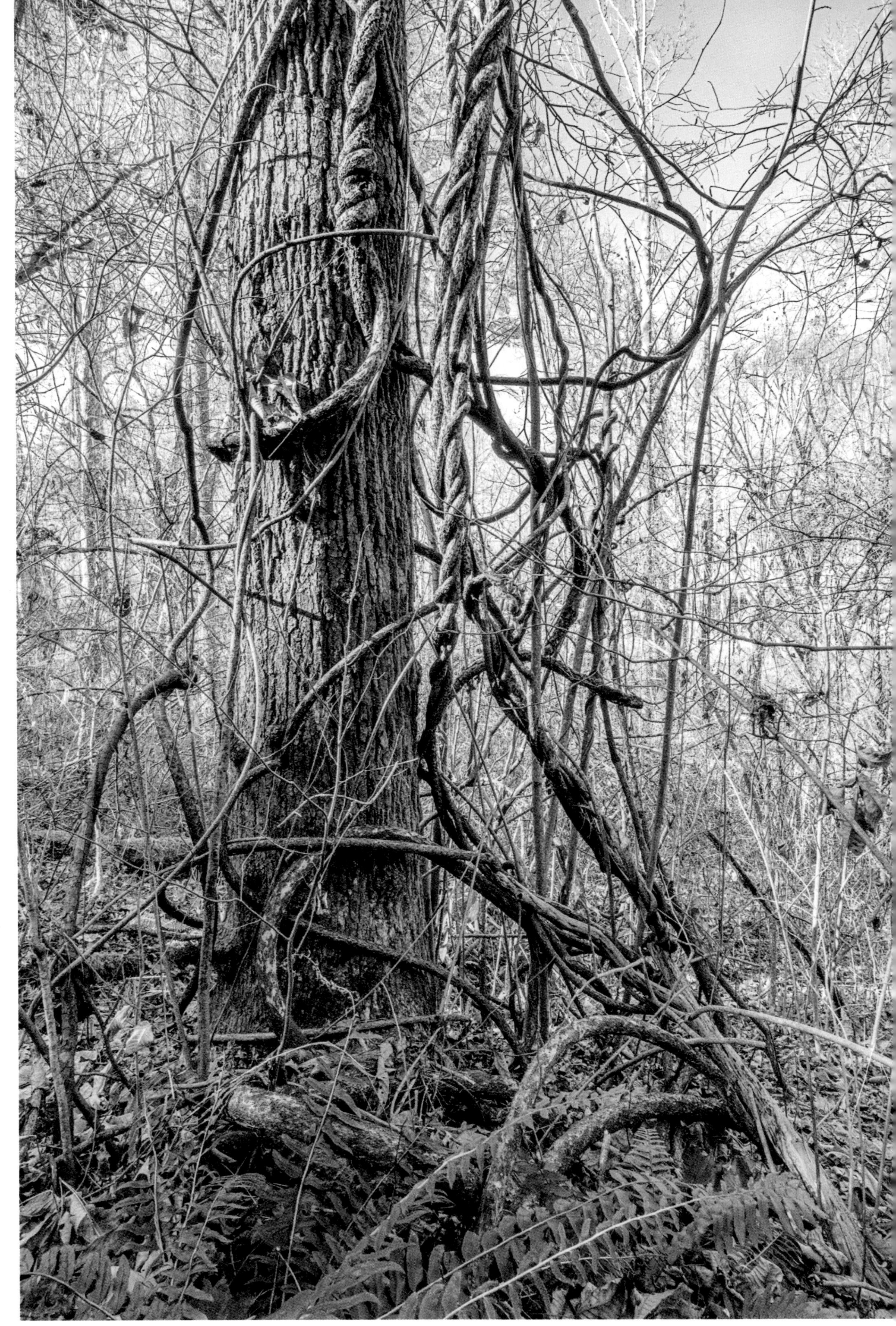

Interstices beckon
Branches, twigs, and twisting vines
Poetry in being

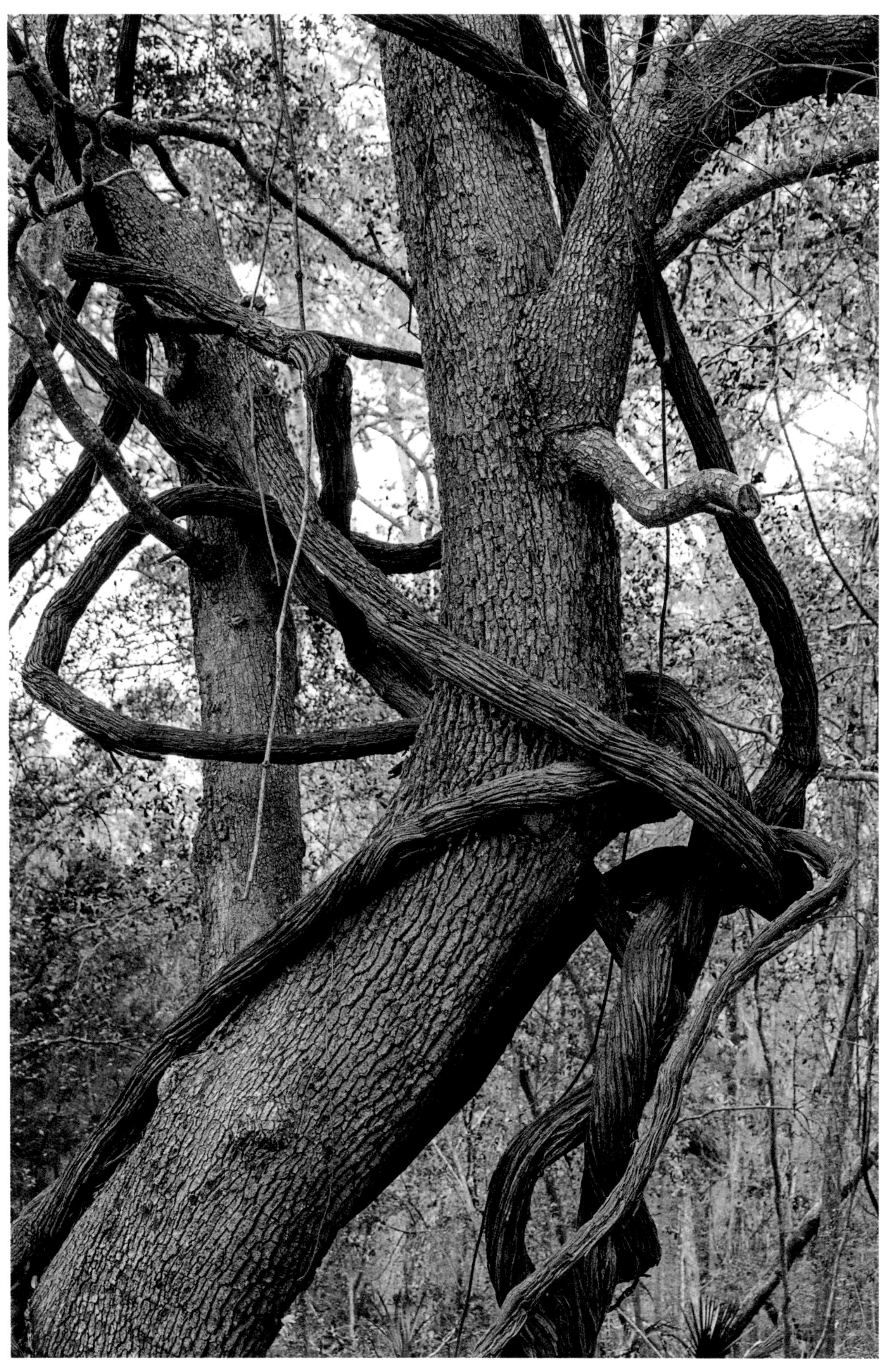

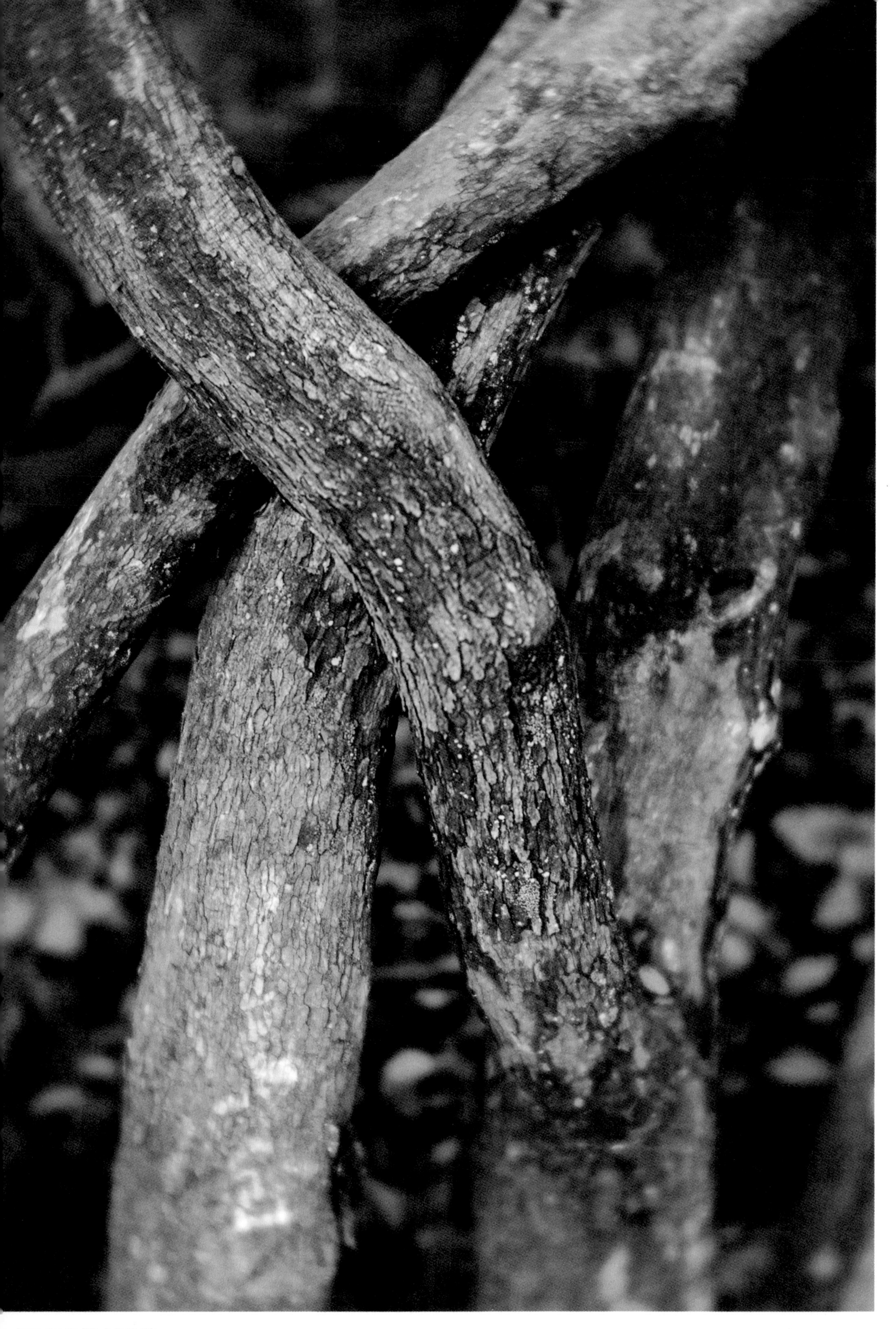

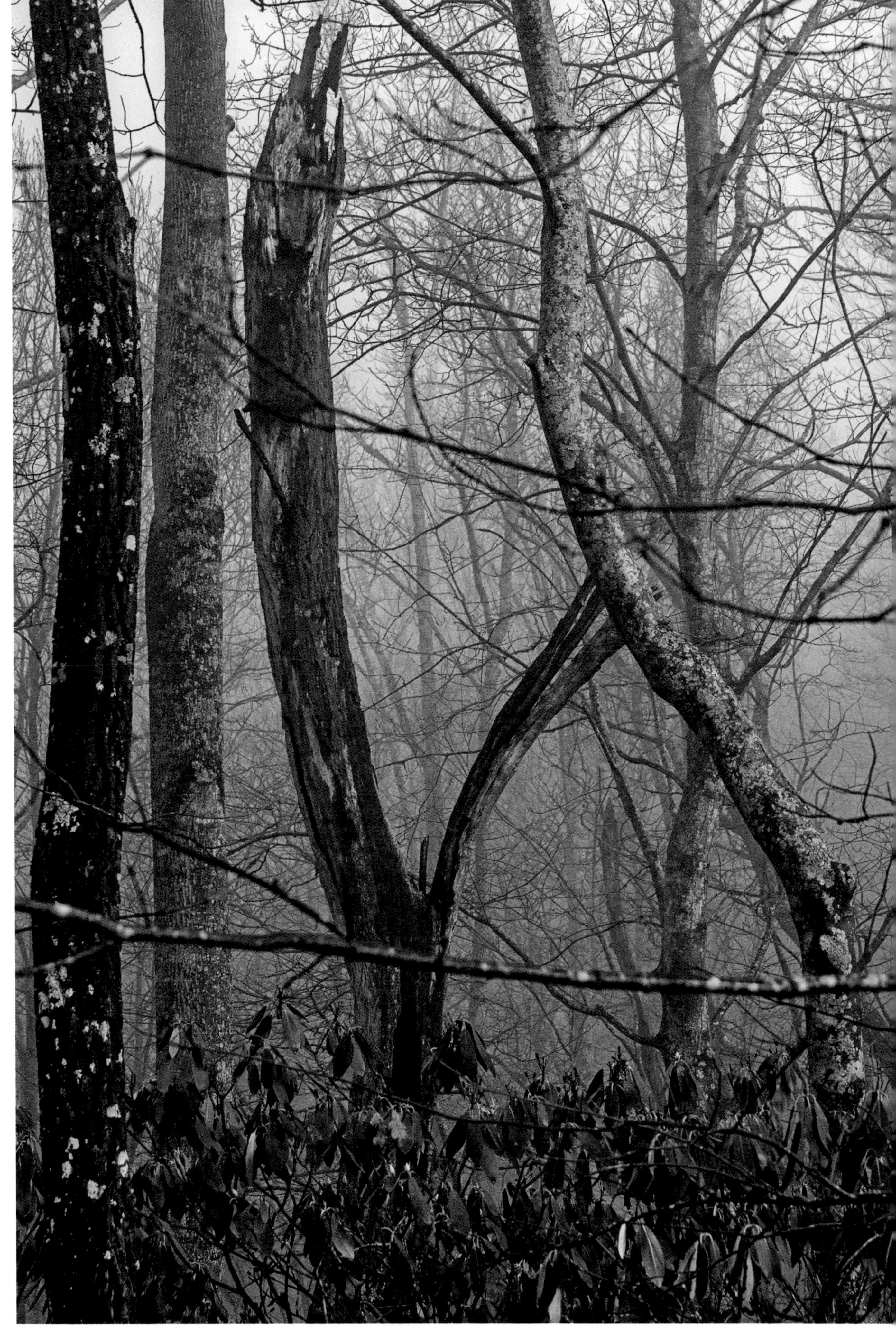

Fissures slice through stone
How much can one heart endure?
Dyssynchrony kills

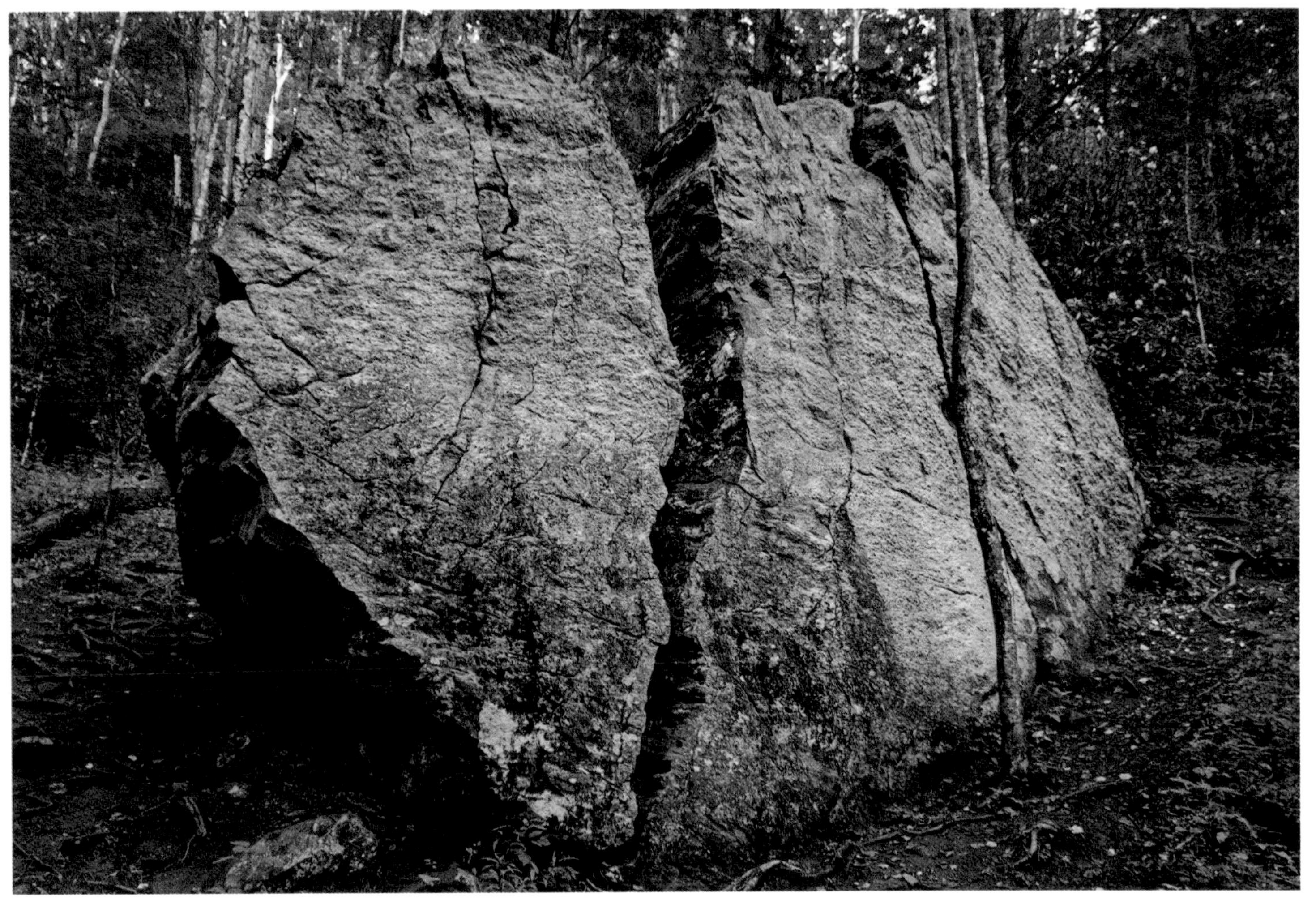

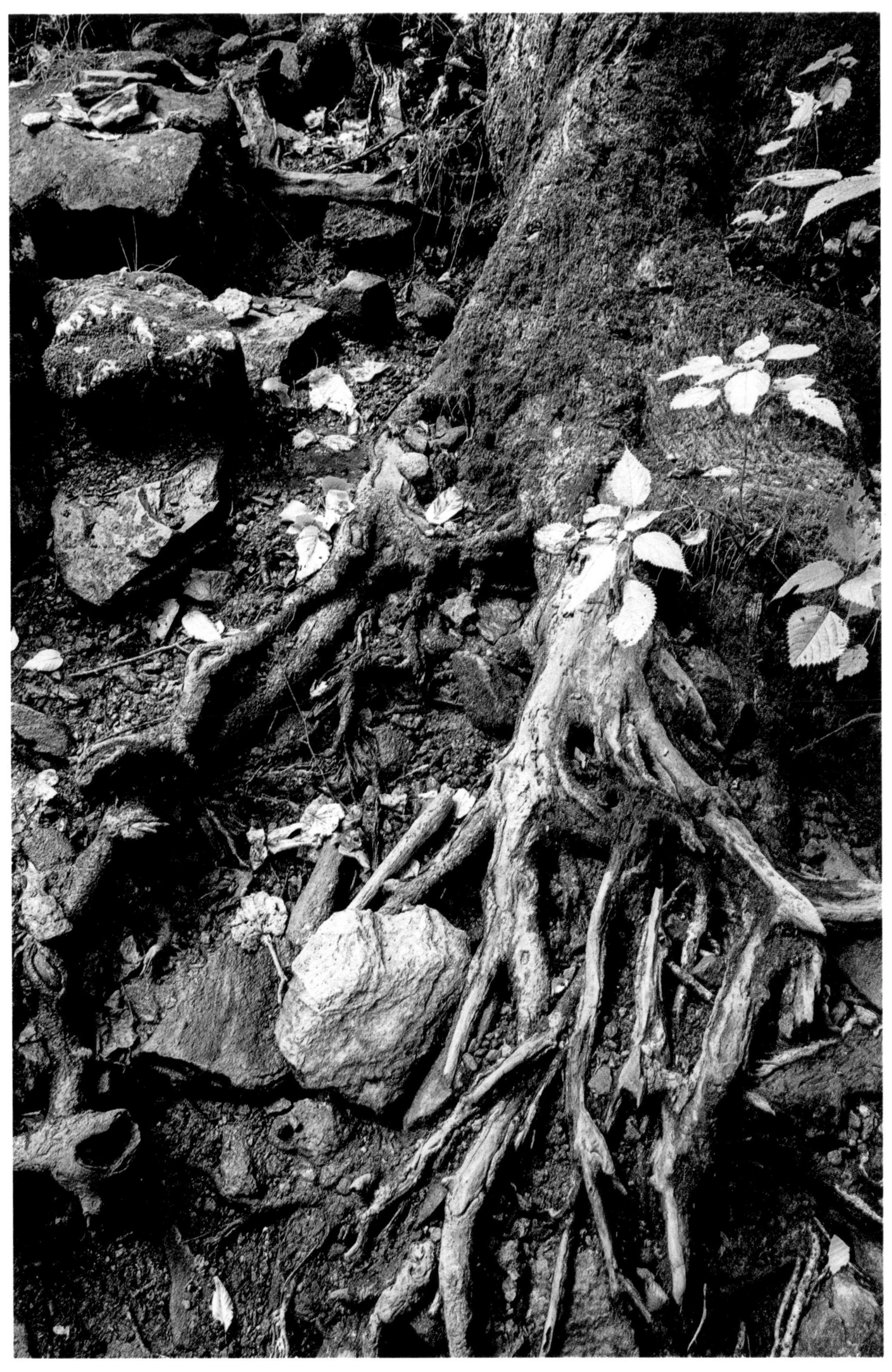

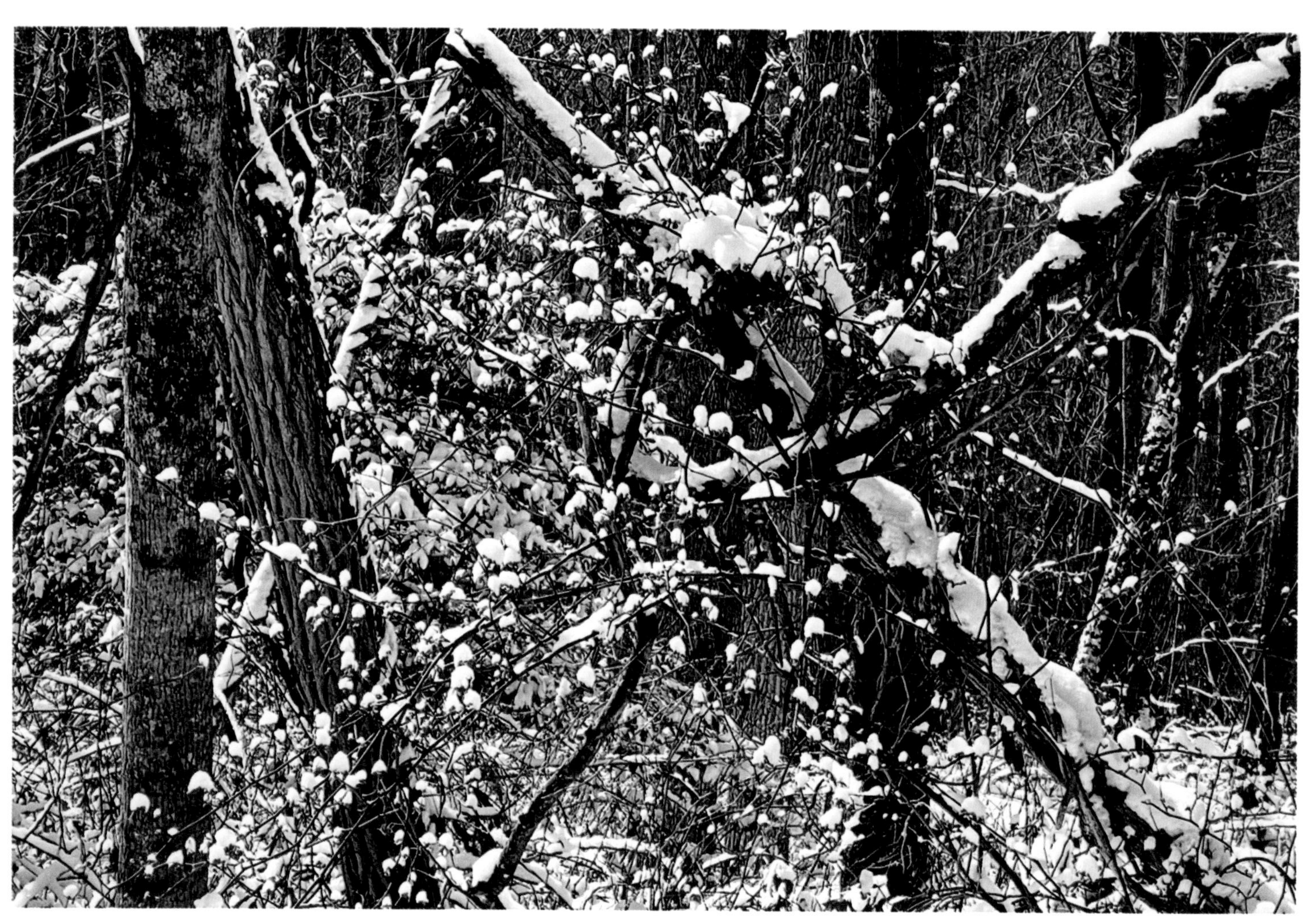

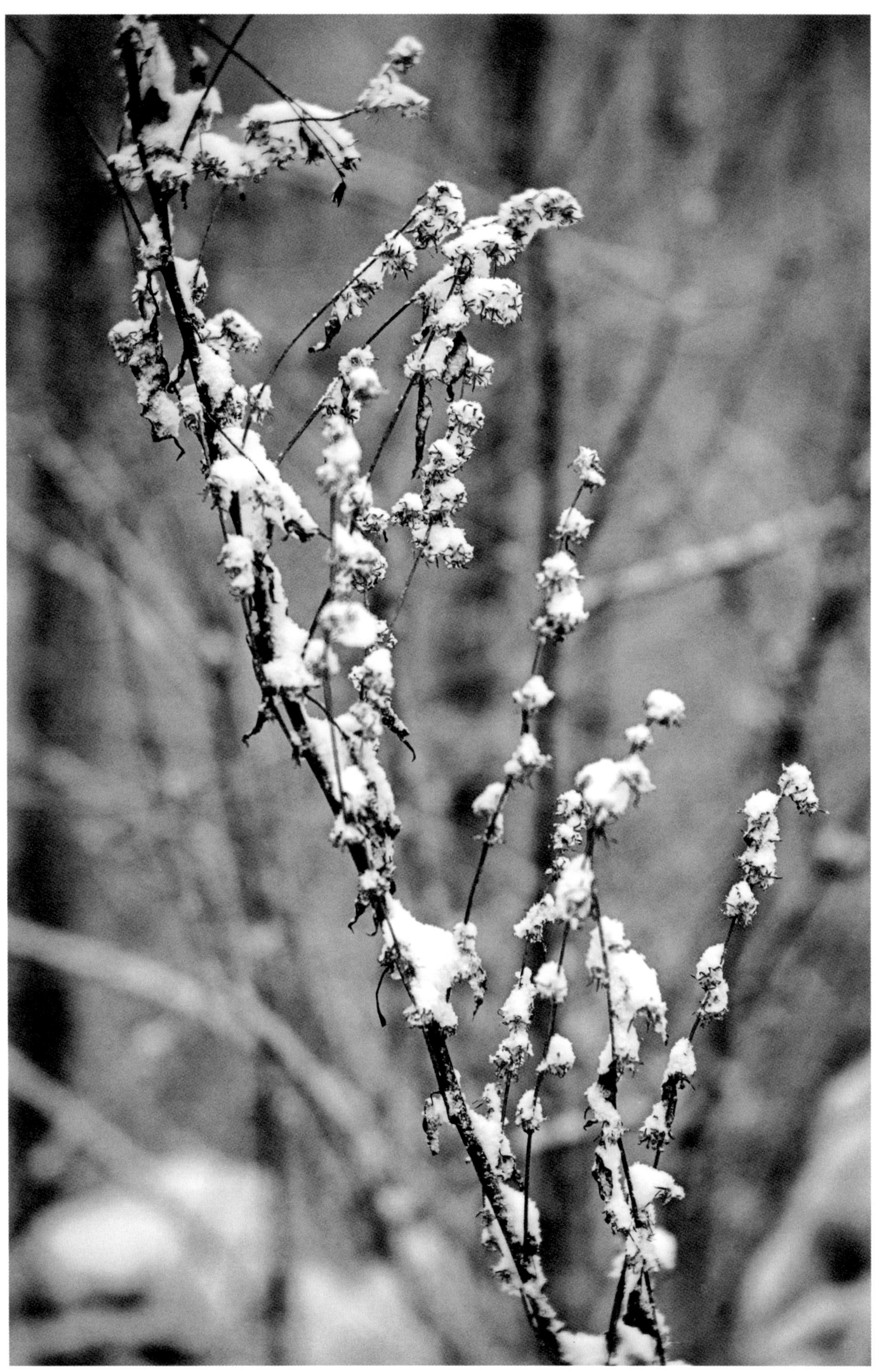

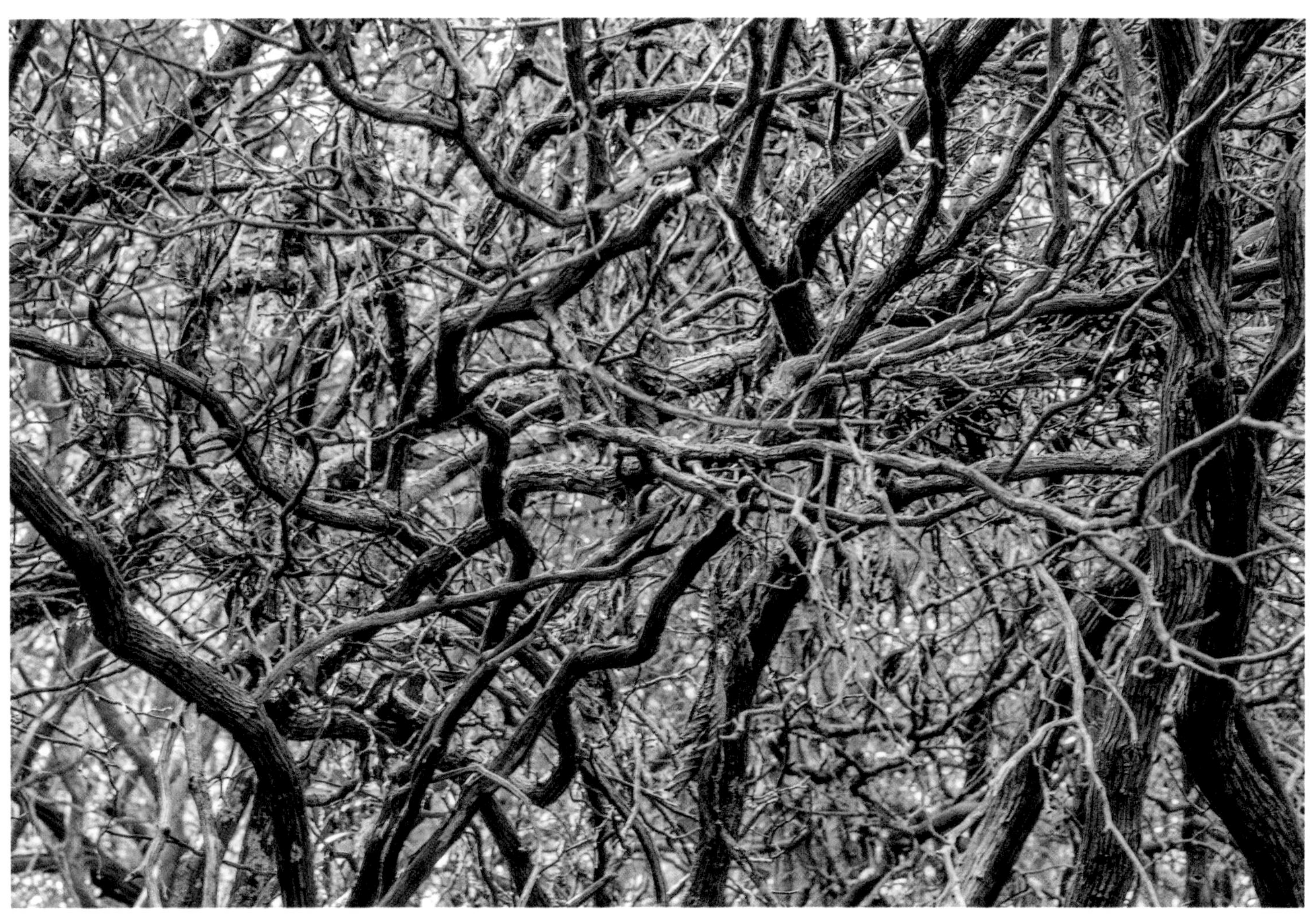

Inside looking out
A man-made maze of branches
Protection isolates

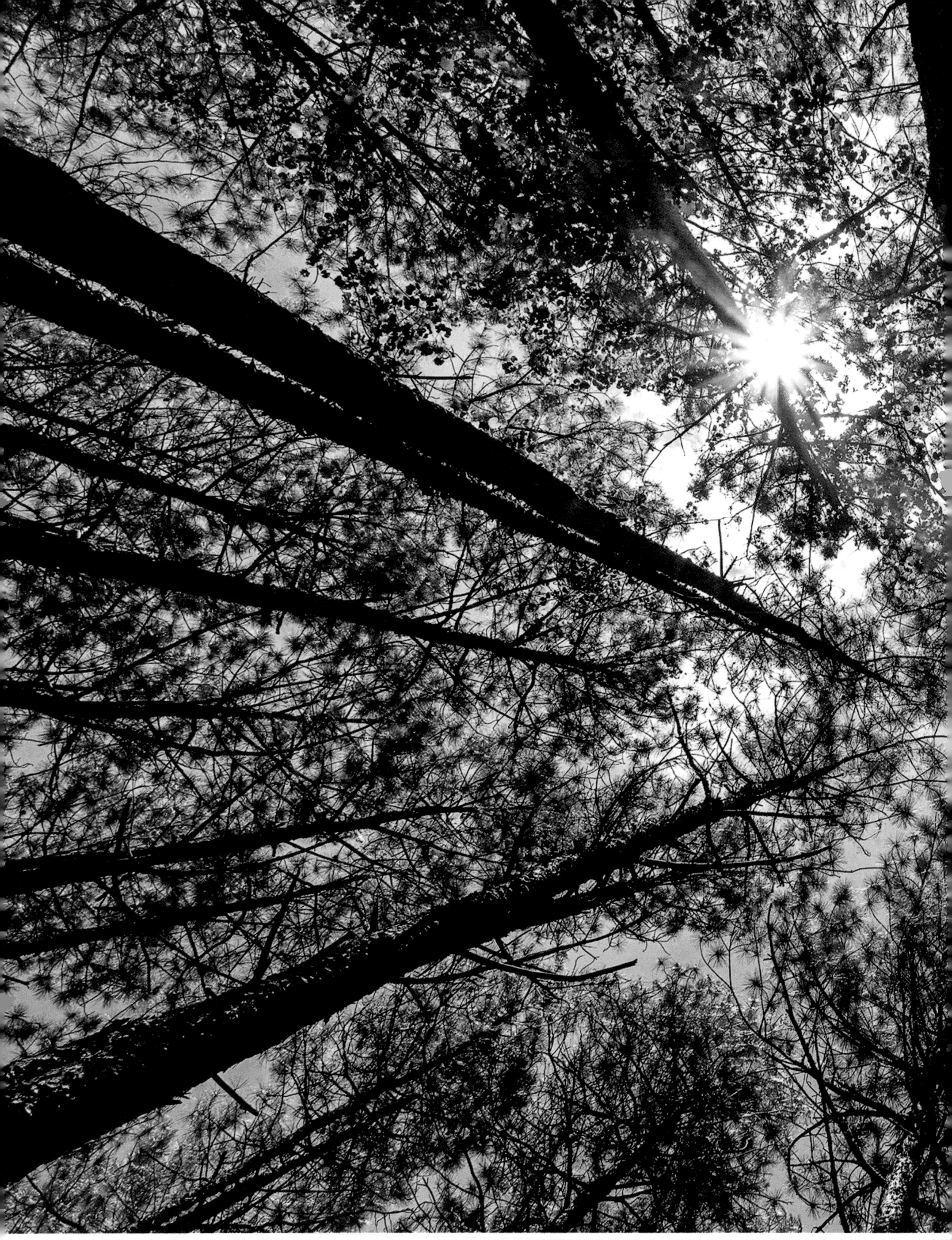

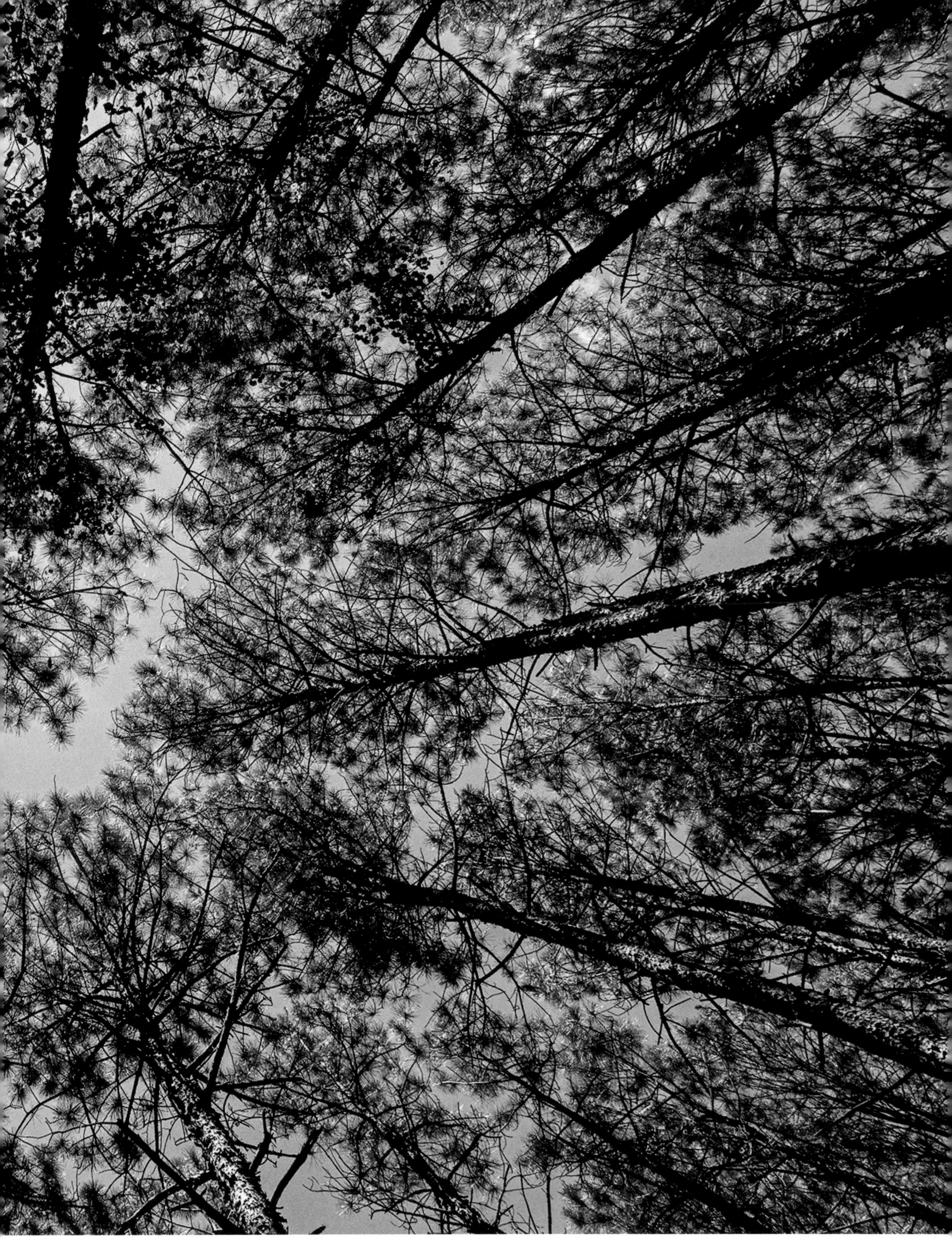

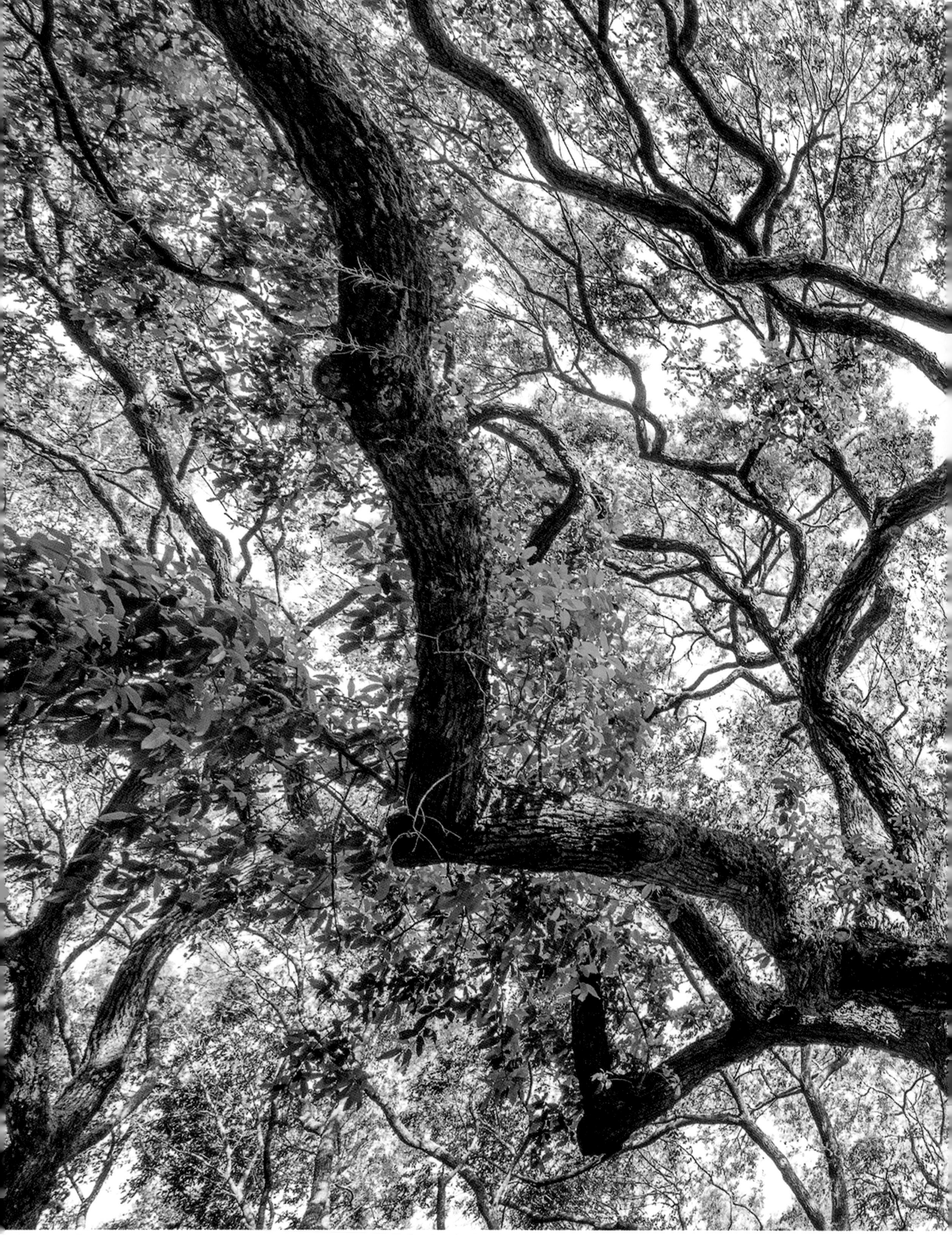

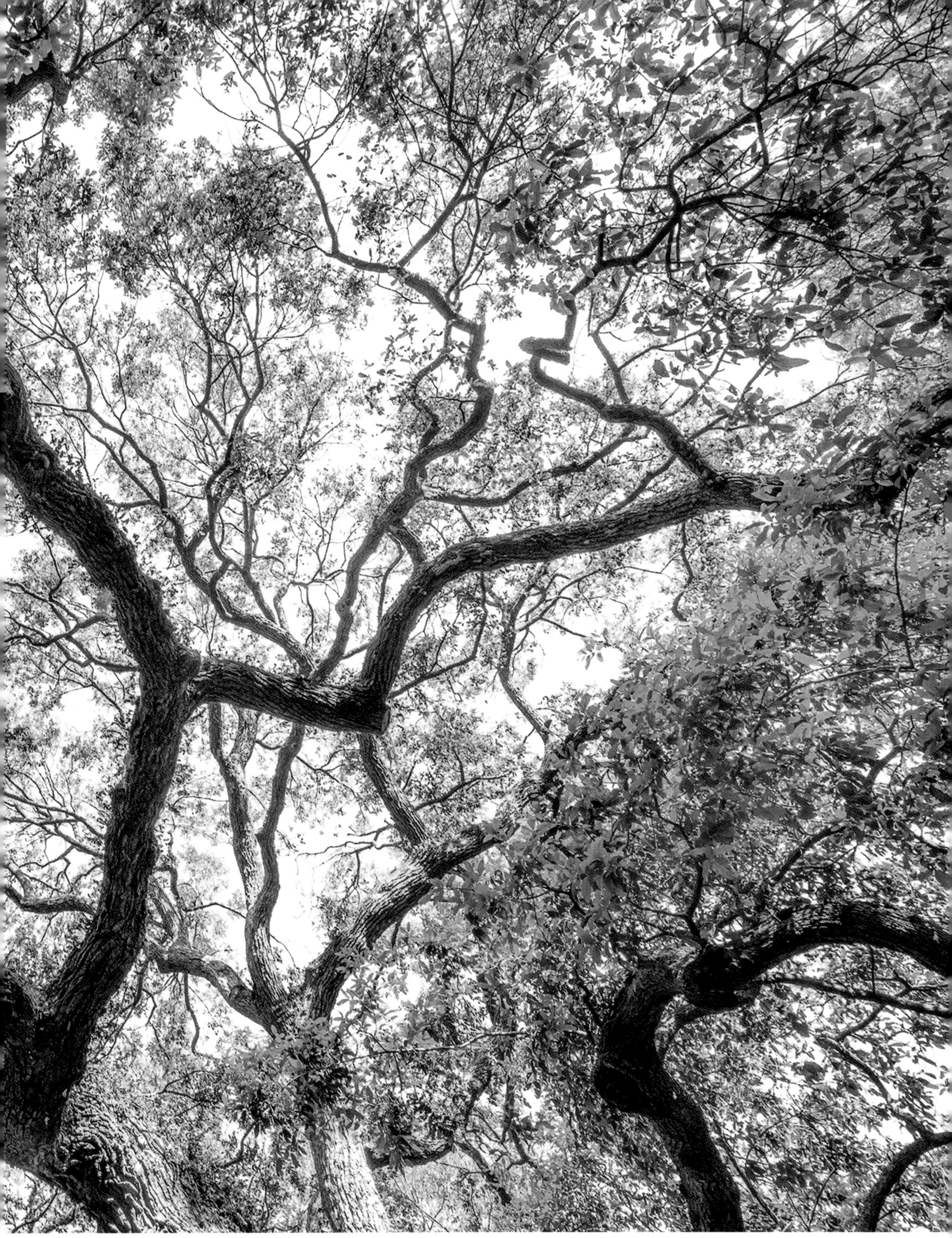

Interior-FIN ofs.indd   85
15.02.2023   15:36

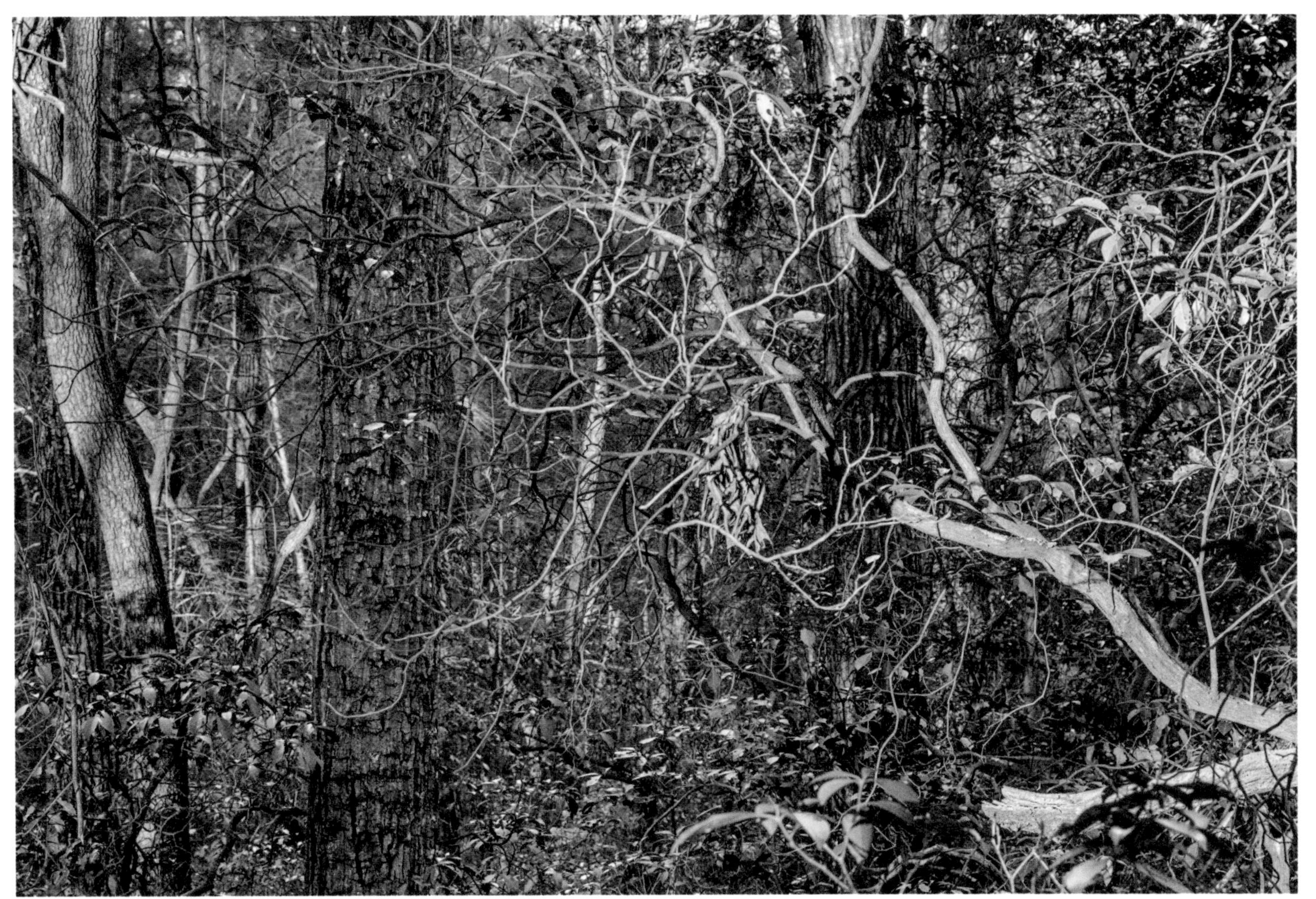

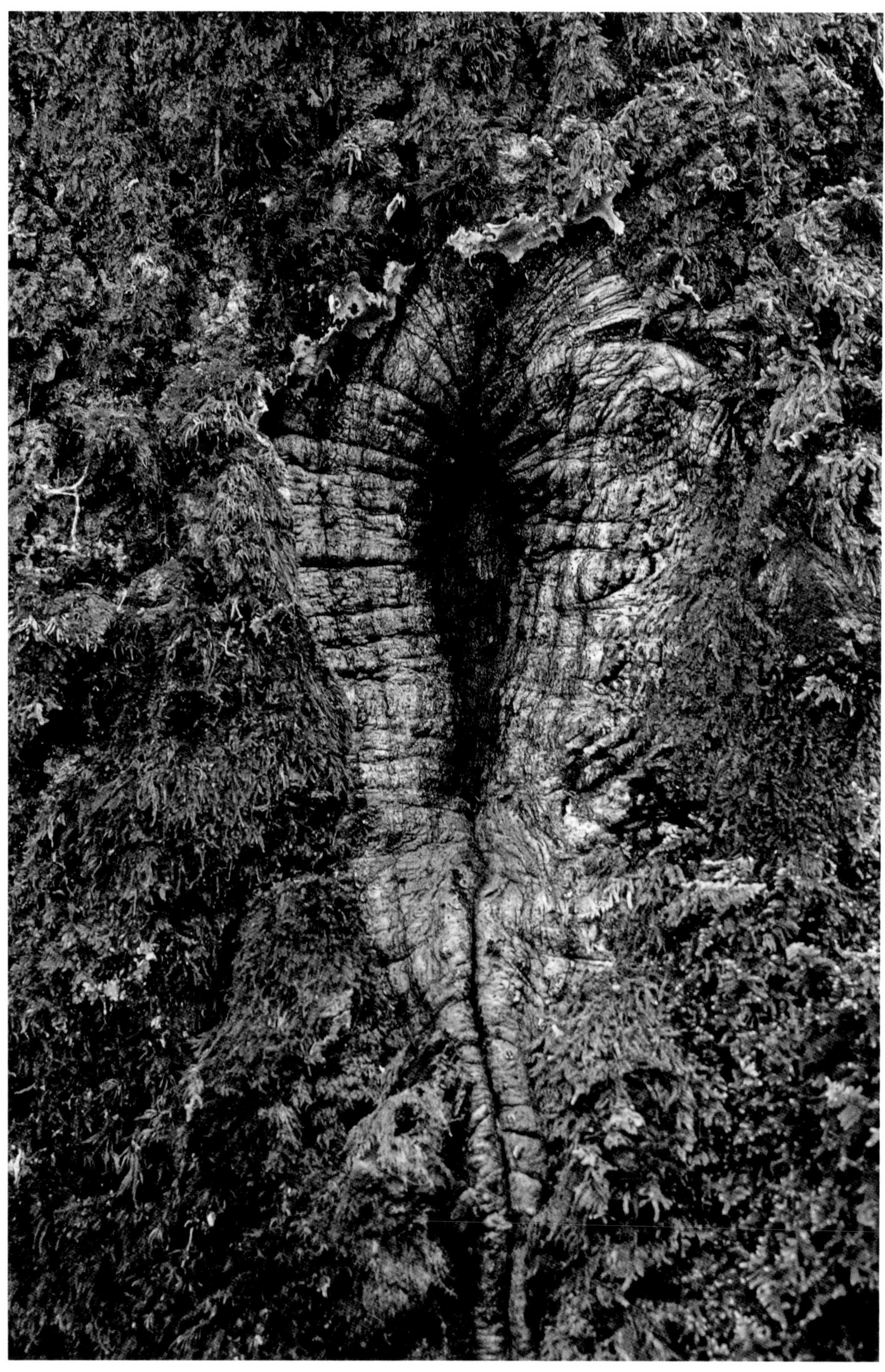

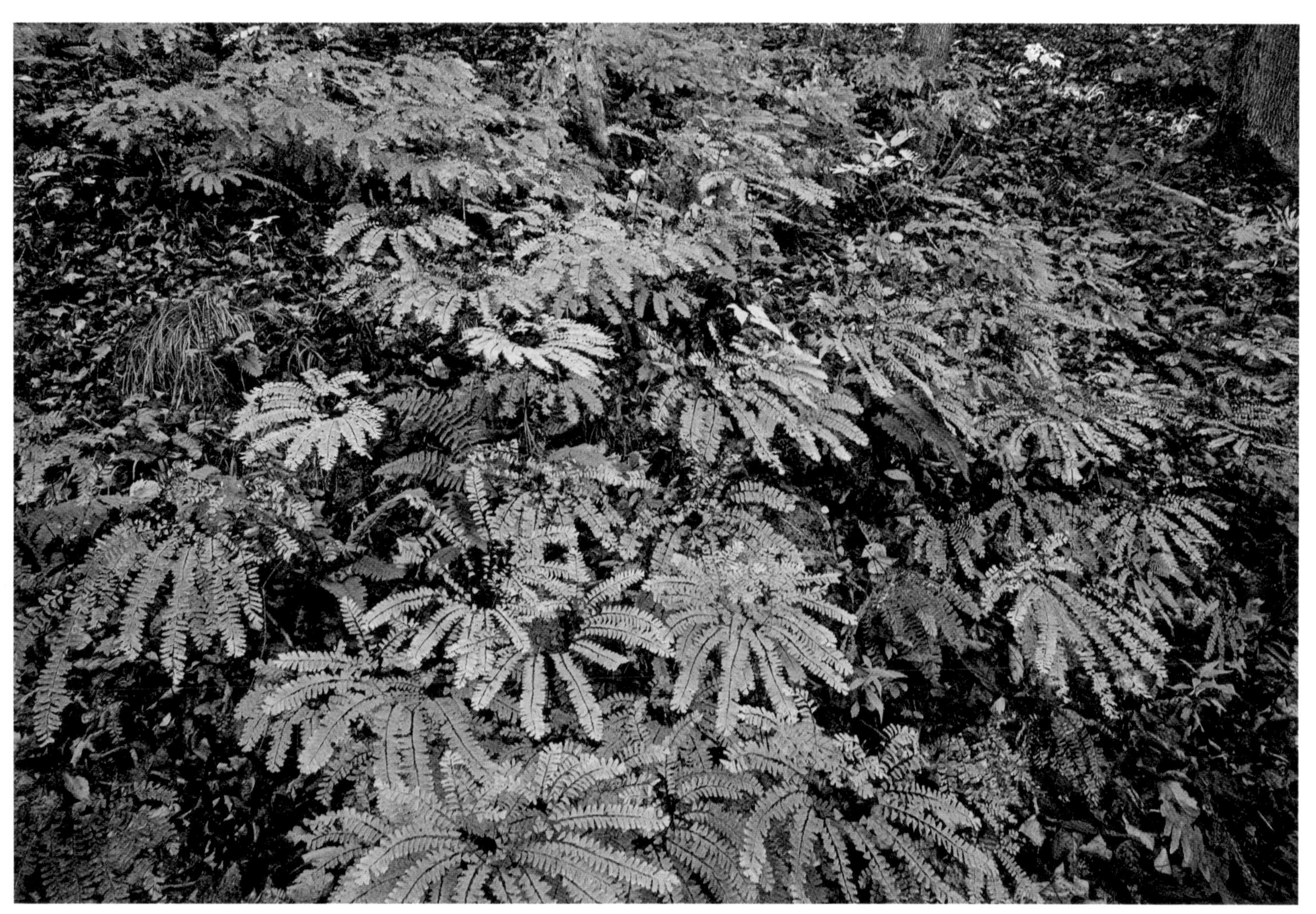

Tiny ice crystals
Drip down ephemerally
A glistening farewell

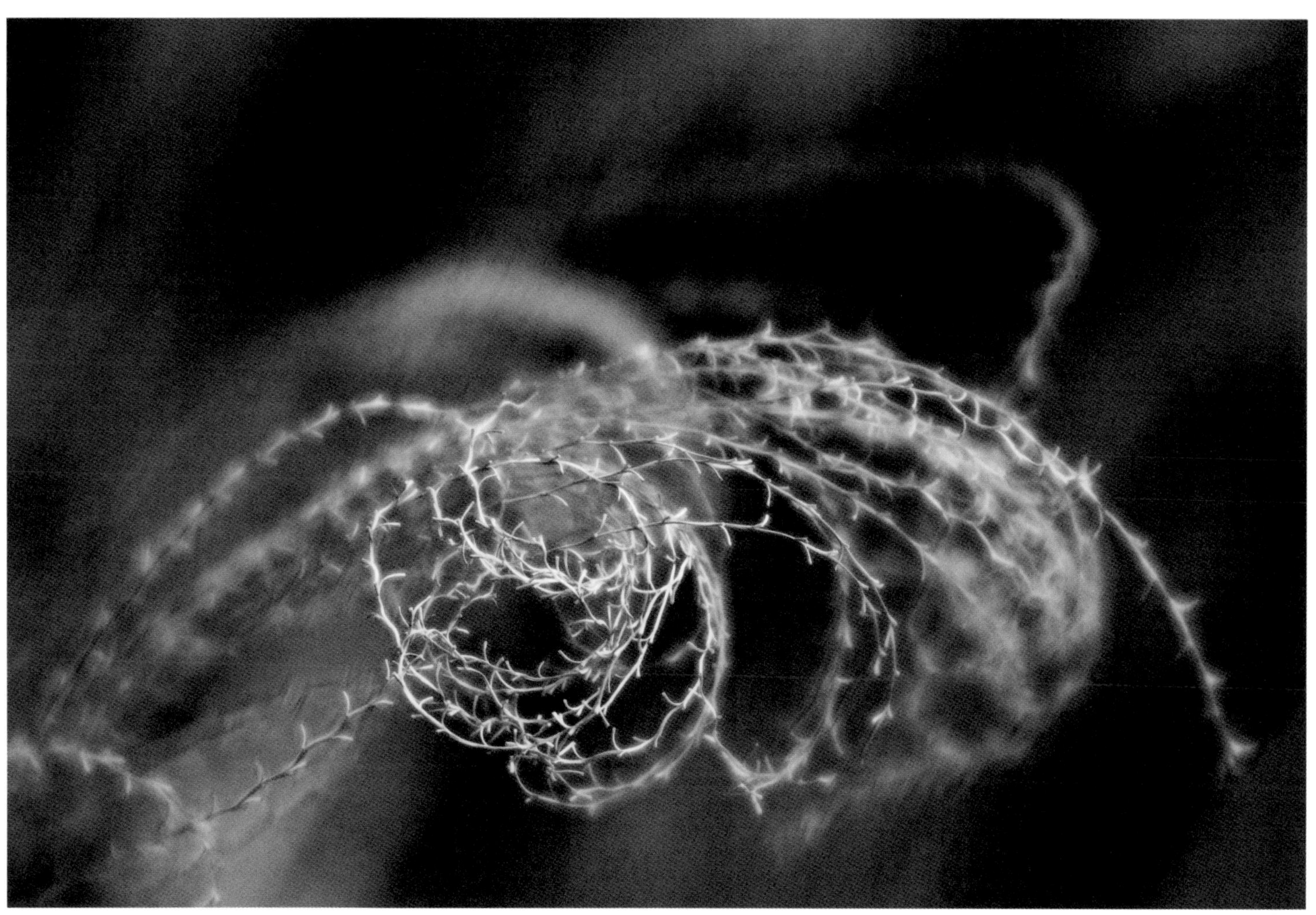

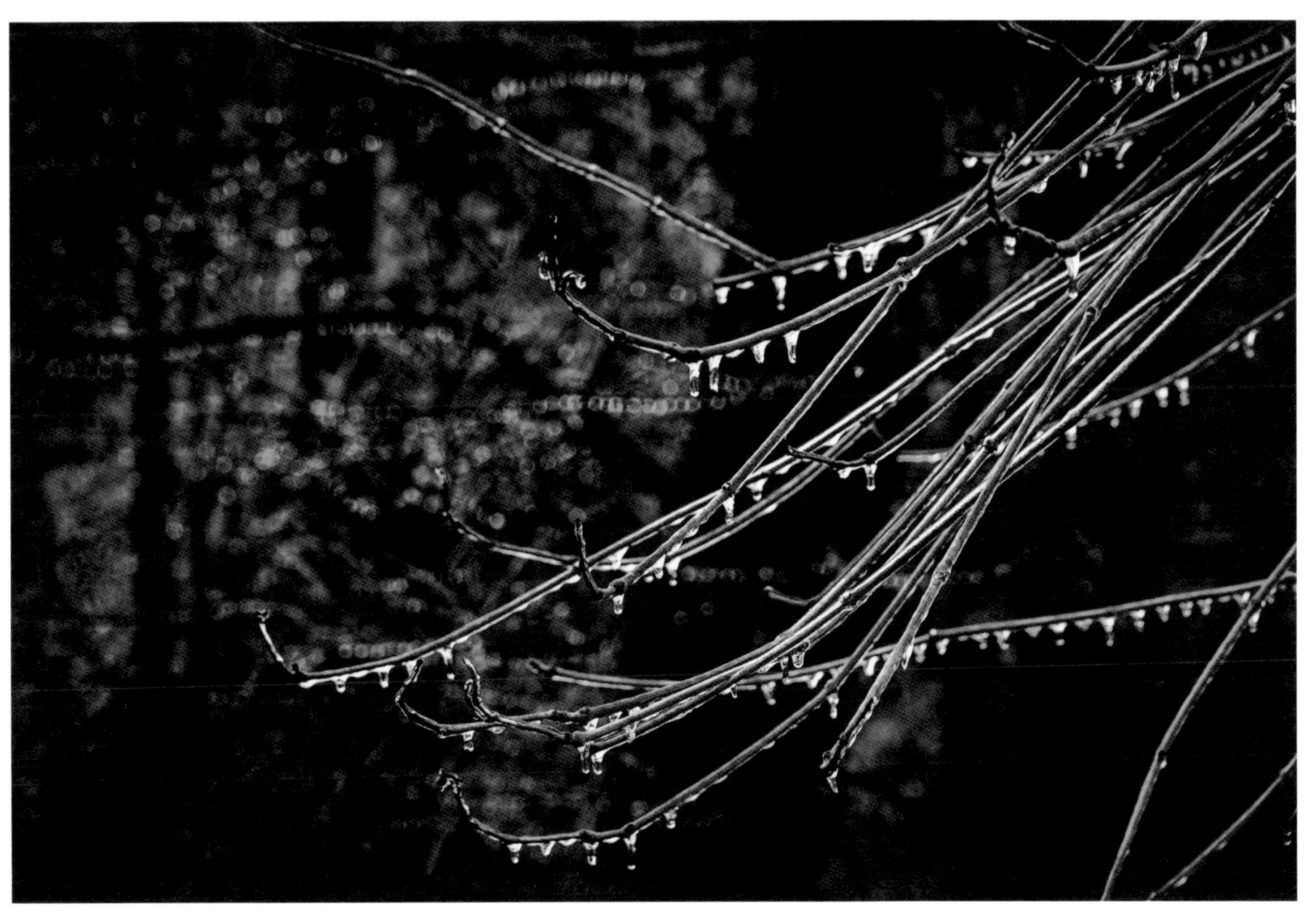

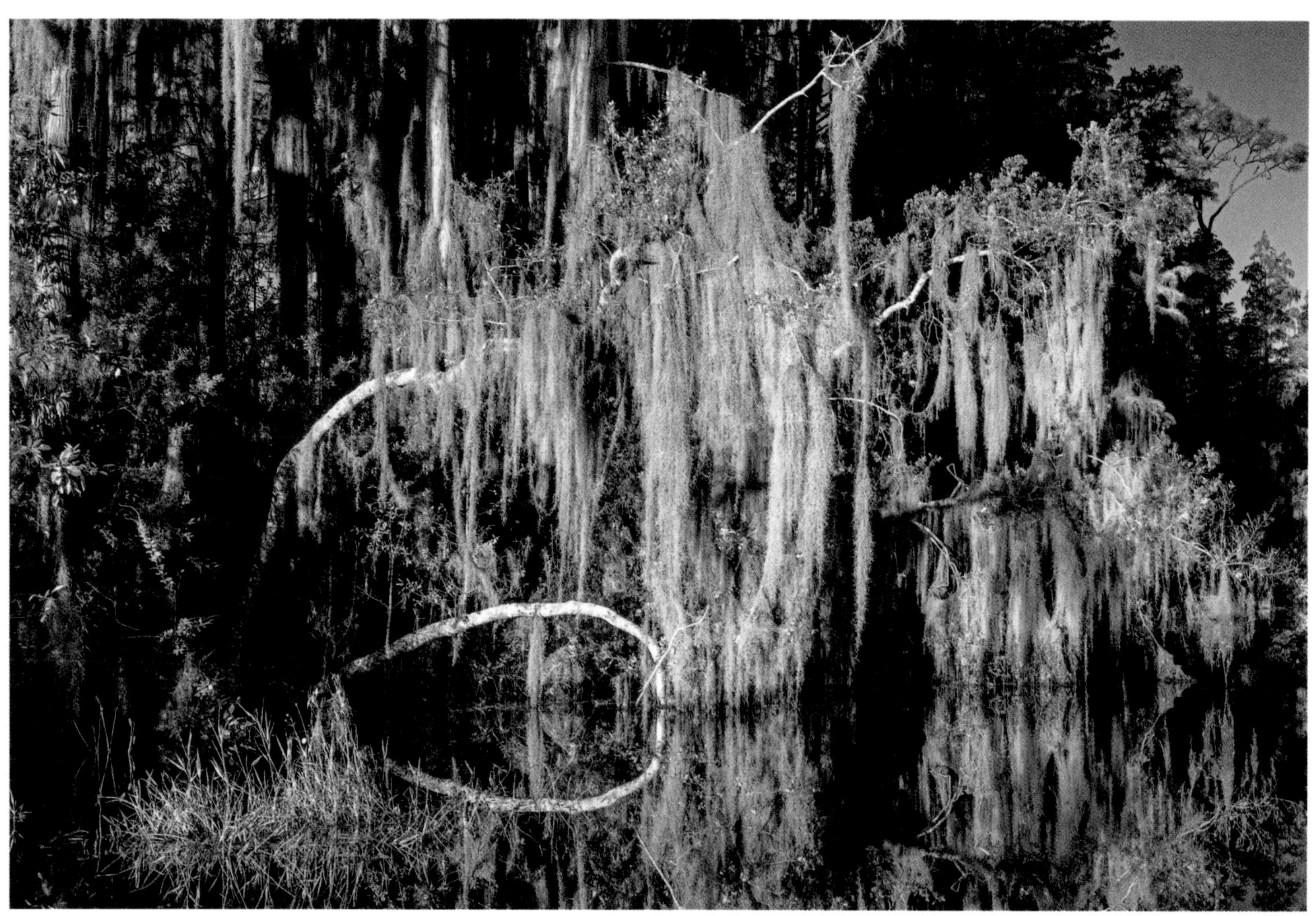

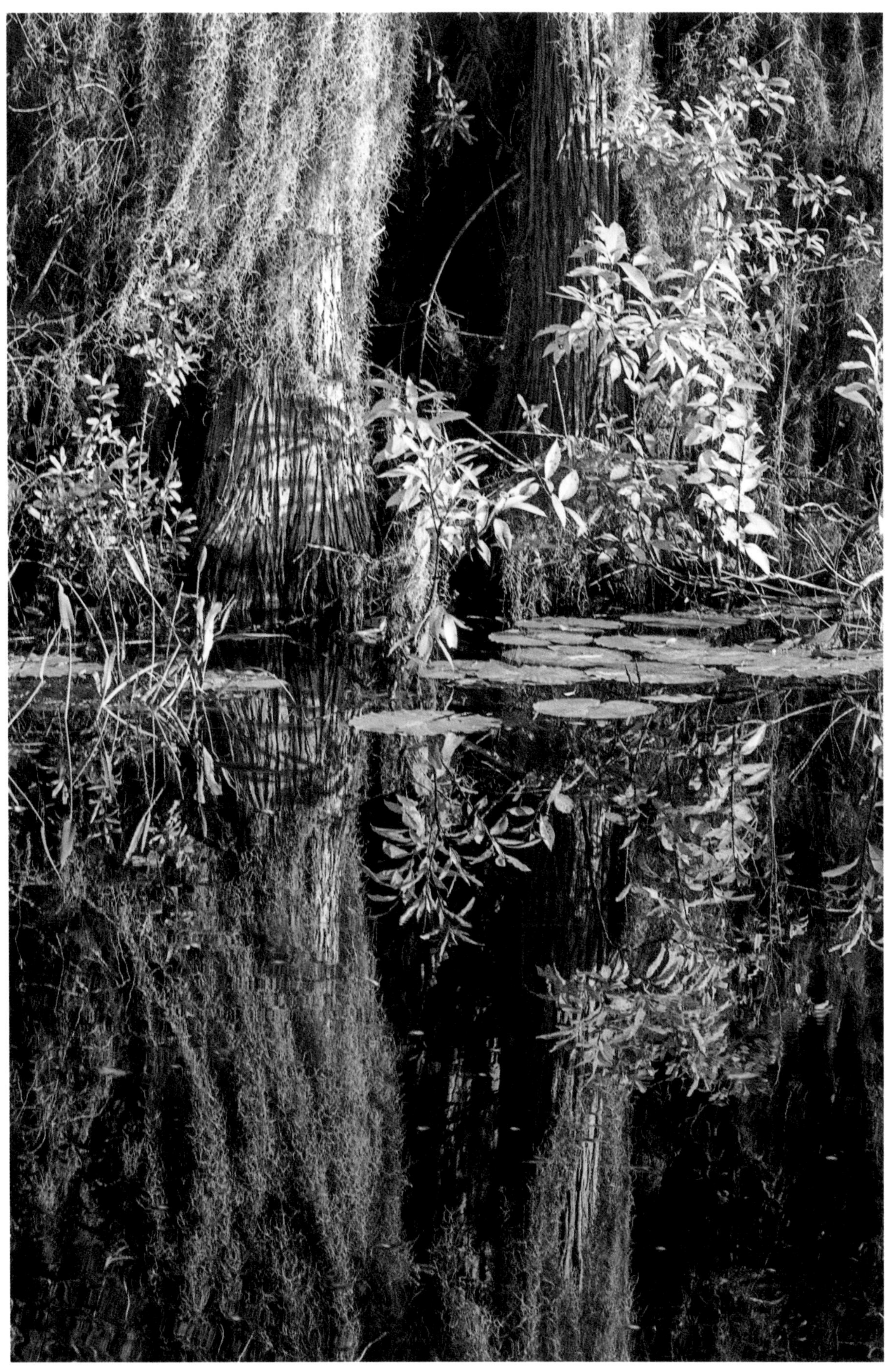

A prairie in the swamp
Jewel-like wildflowers shimmer
Energy abounds

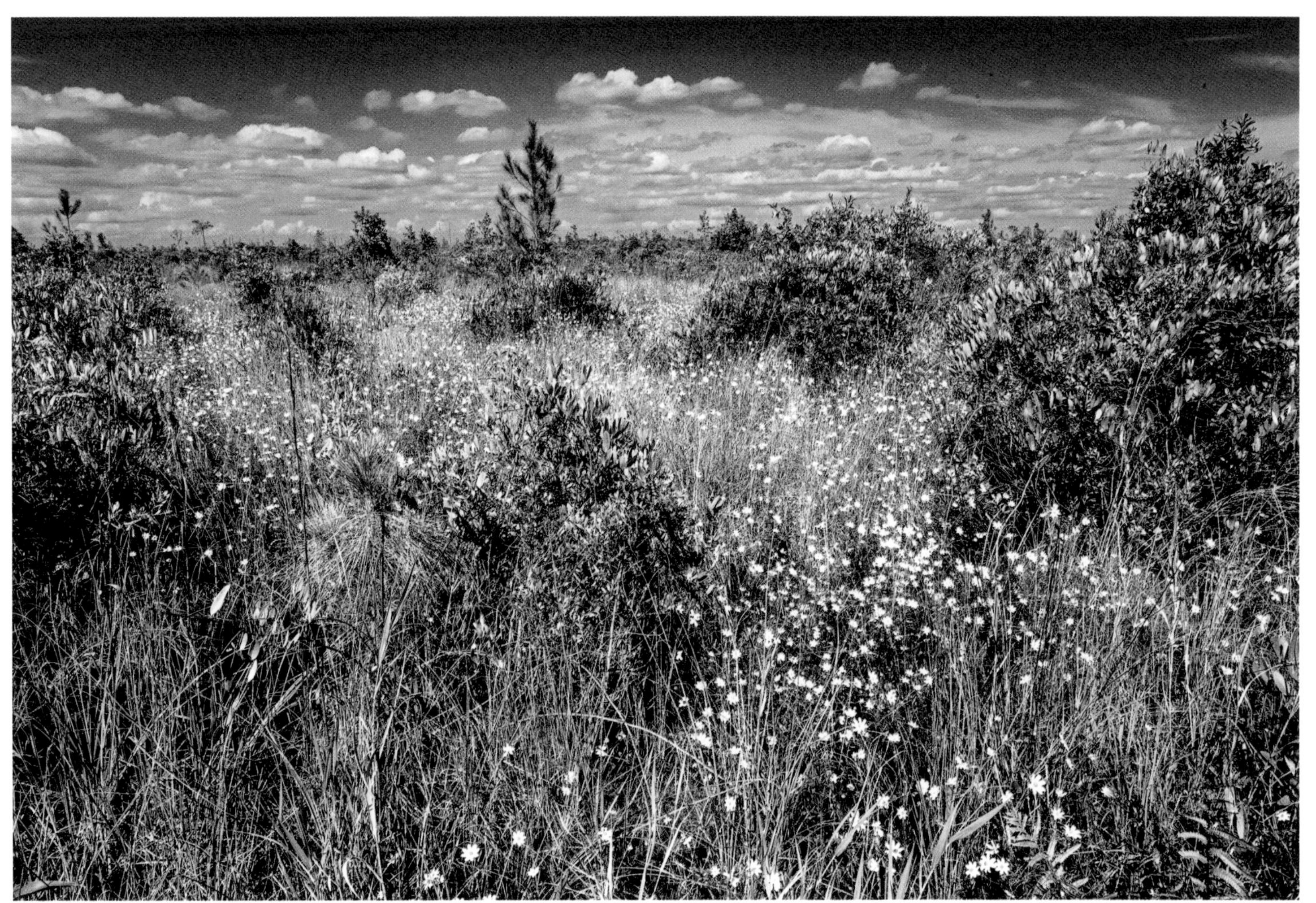

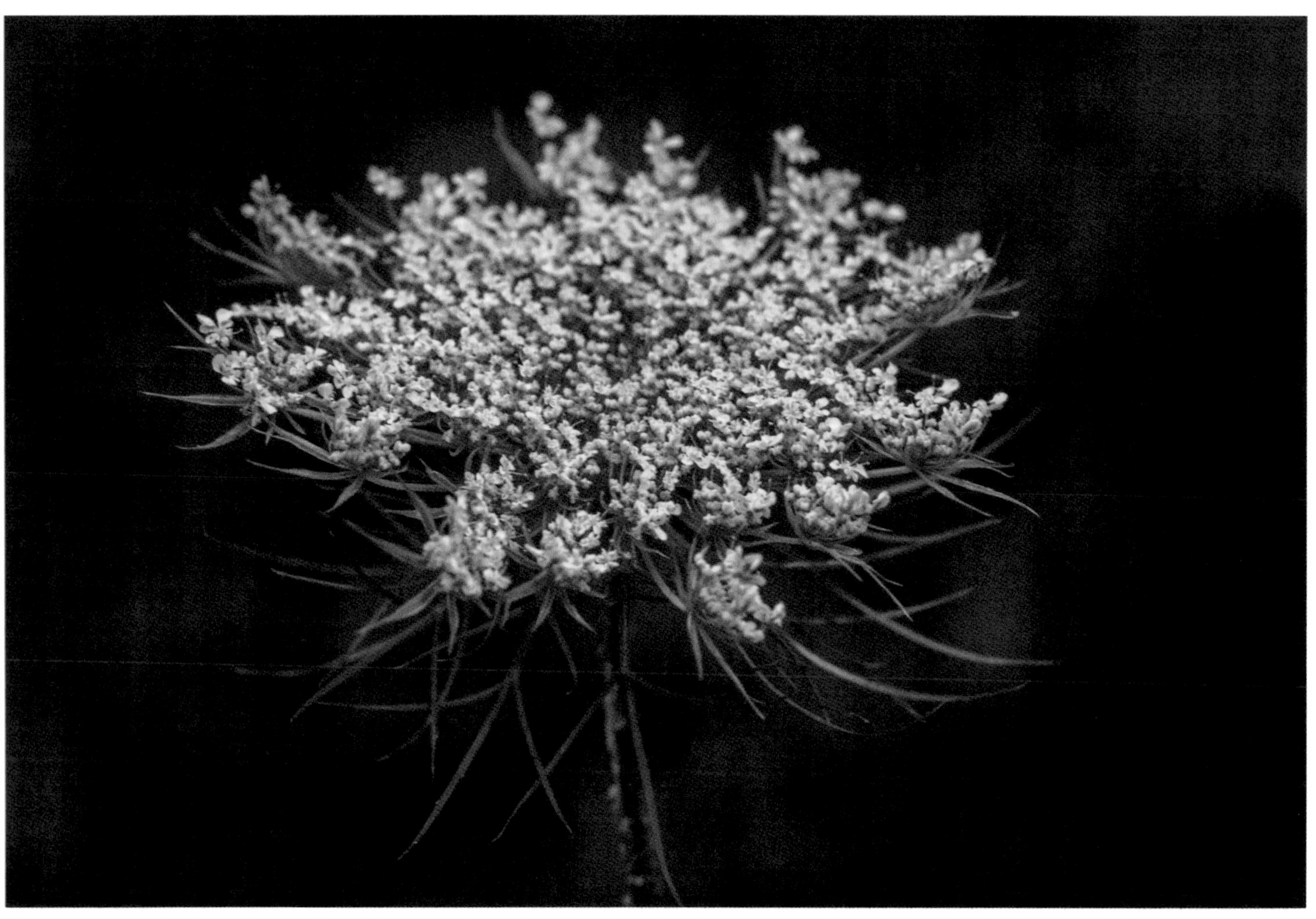

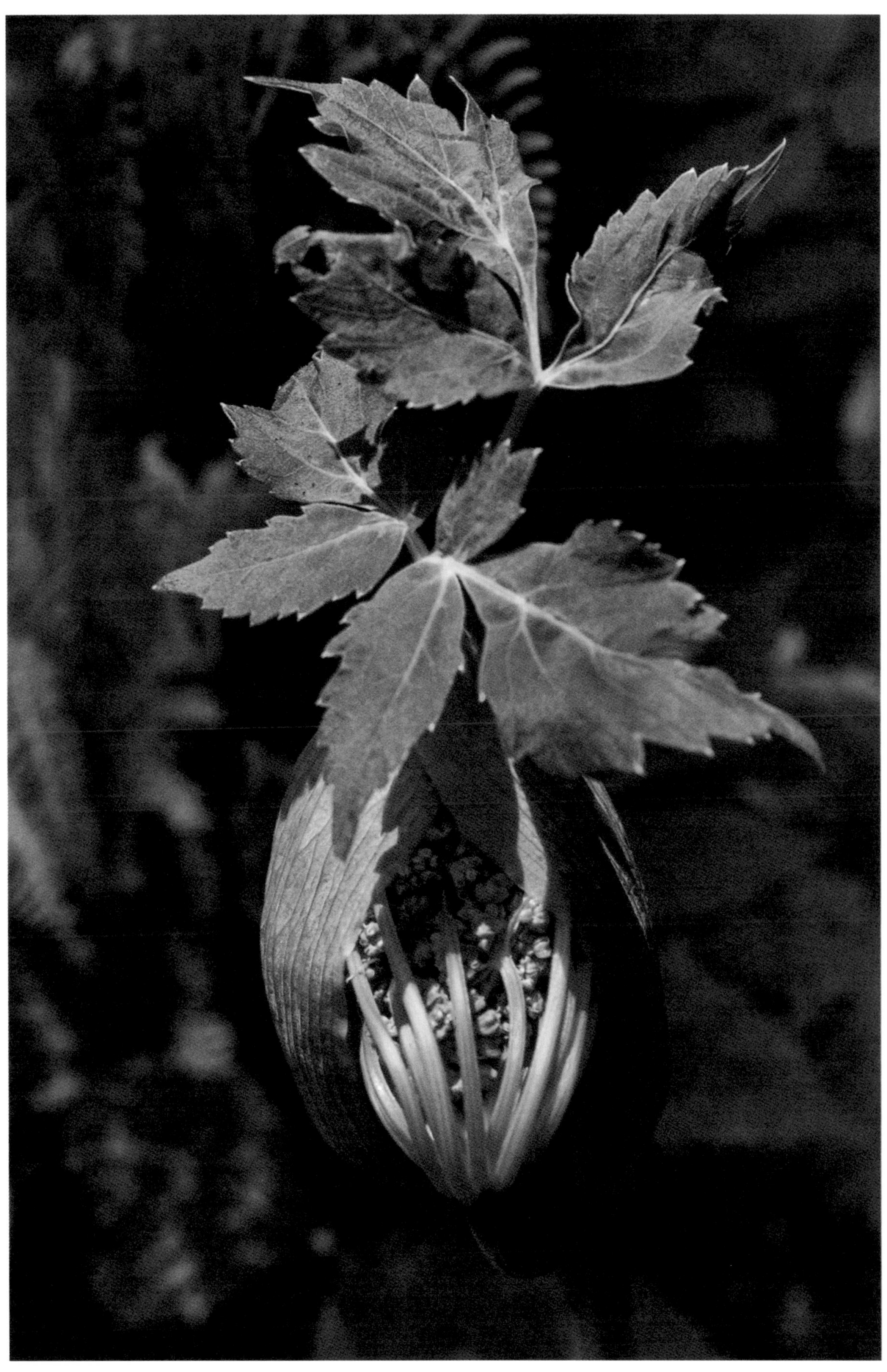

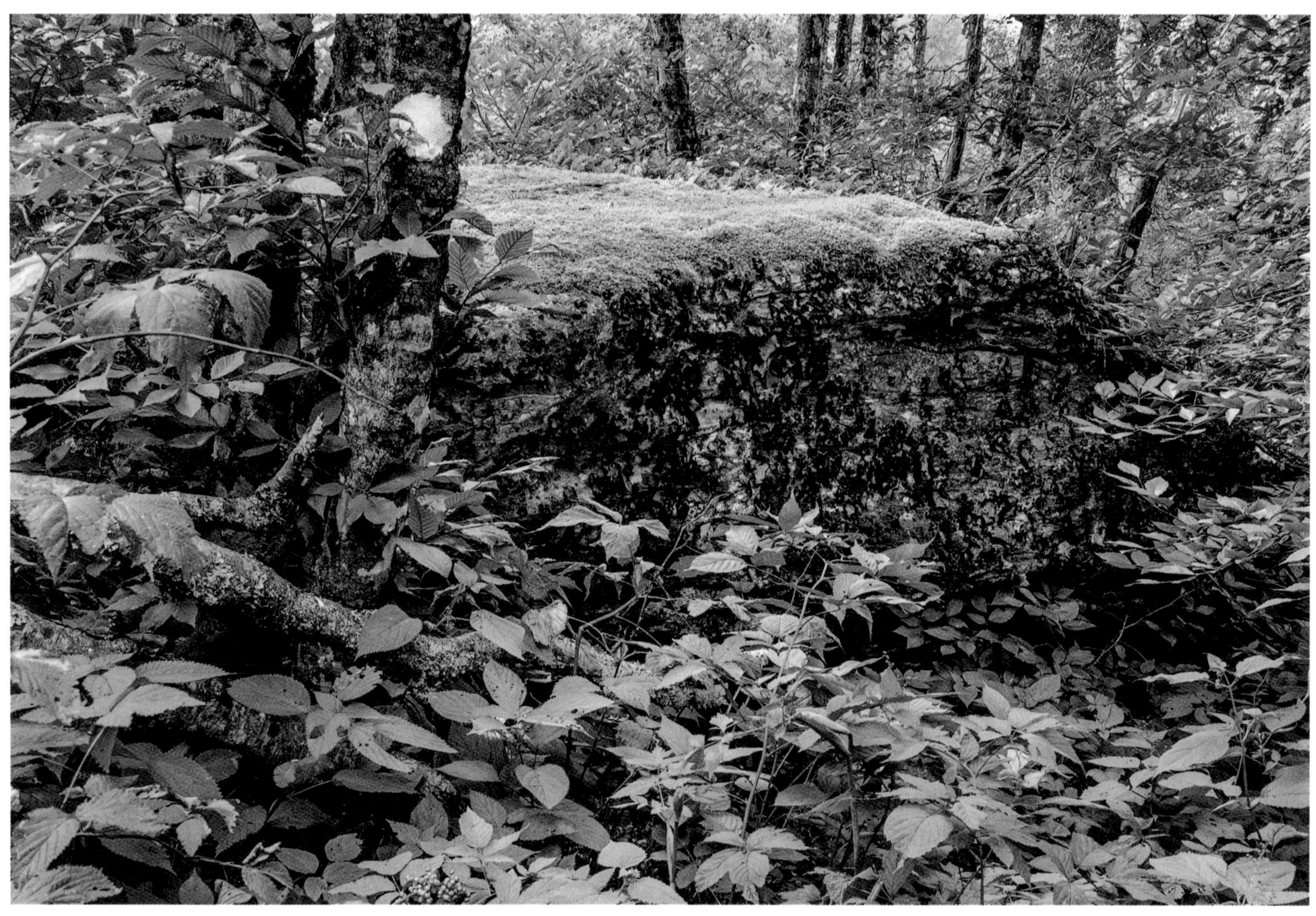

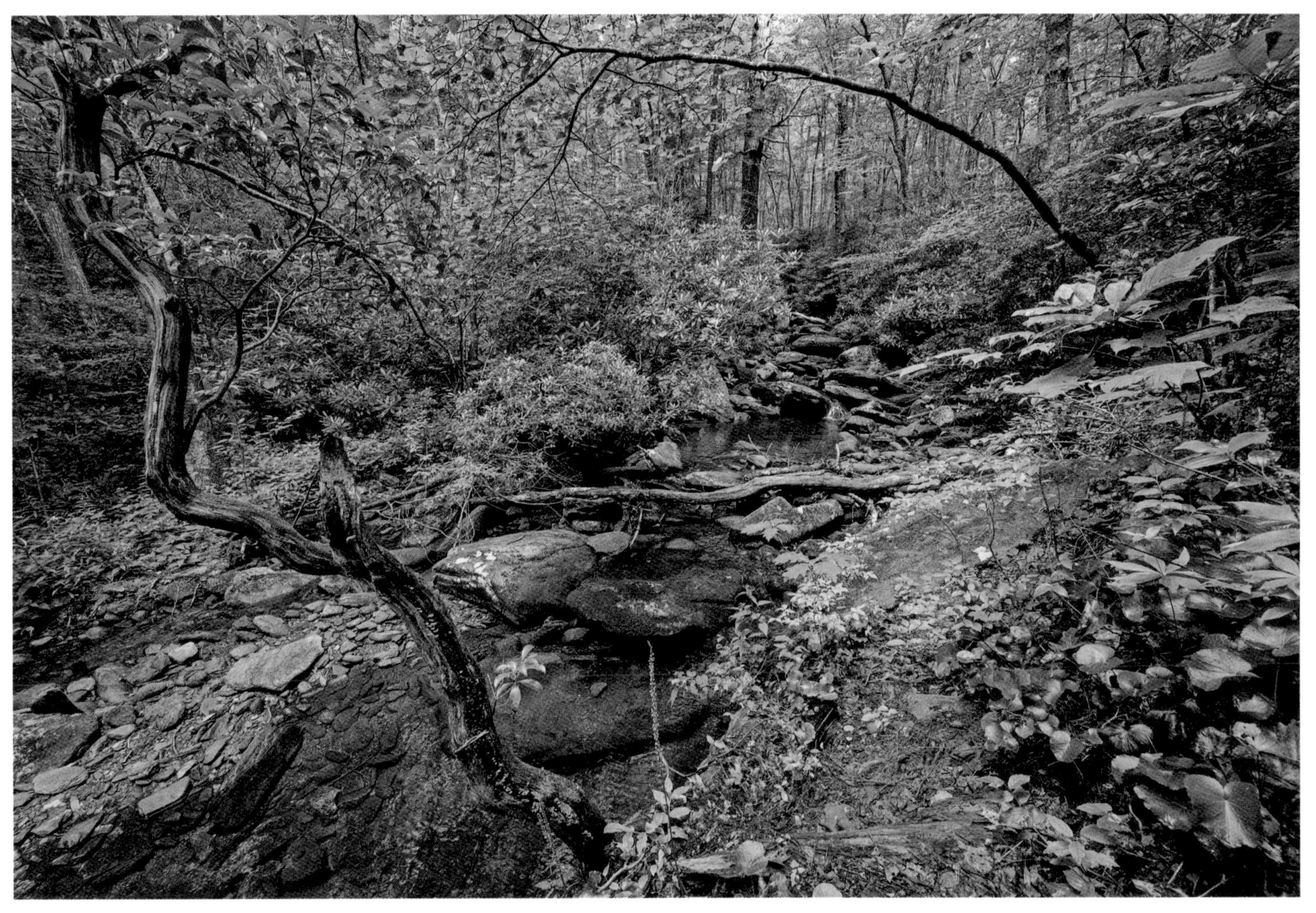

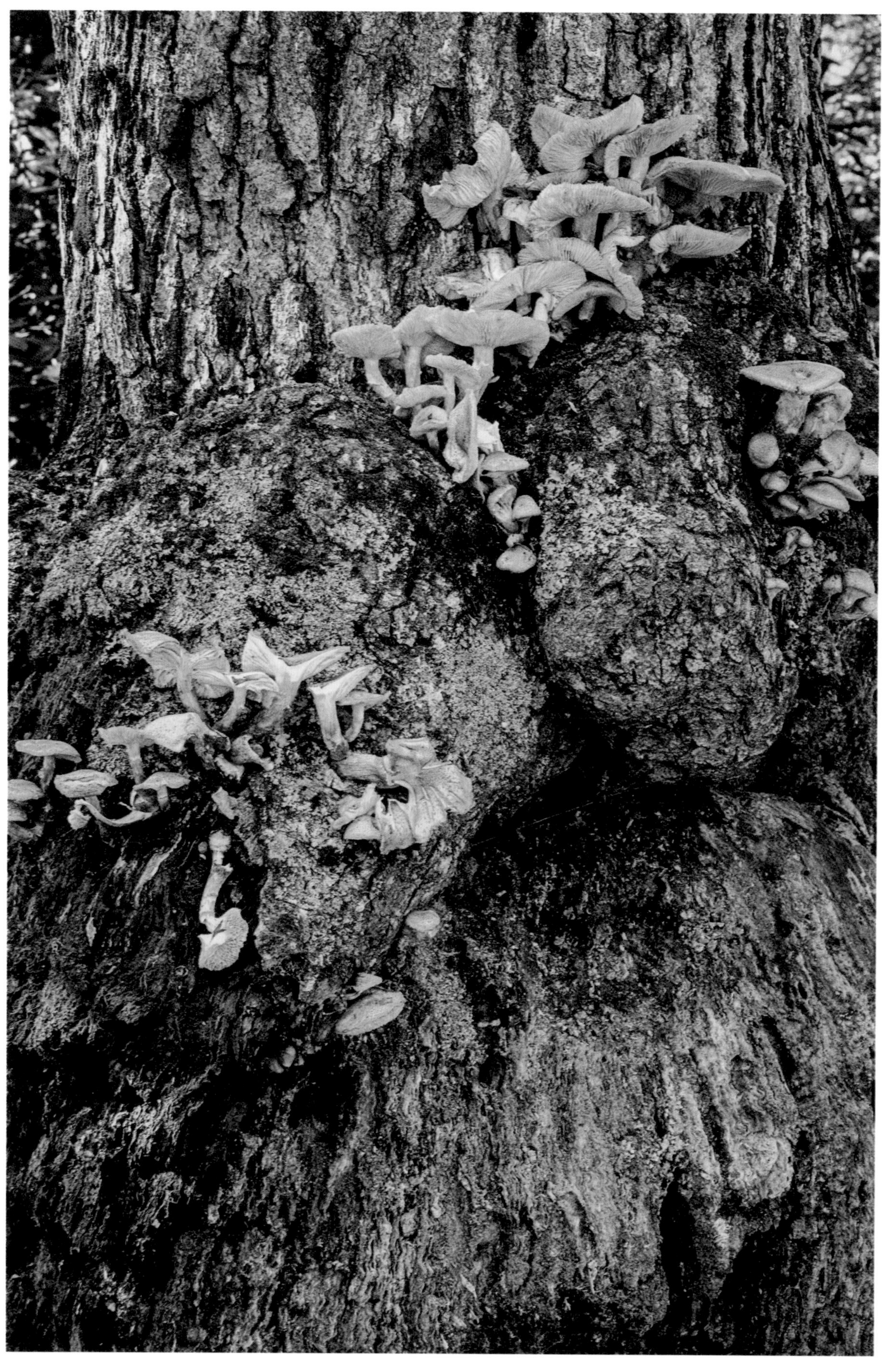

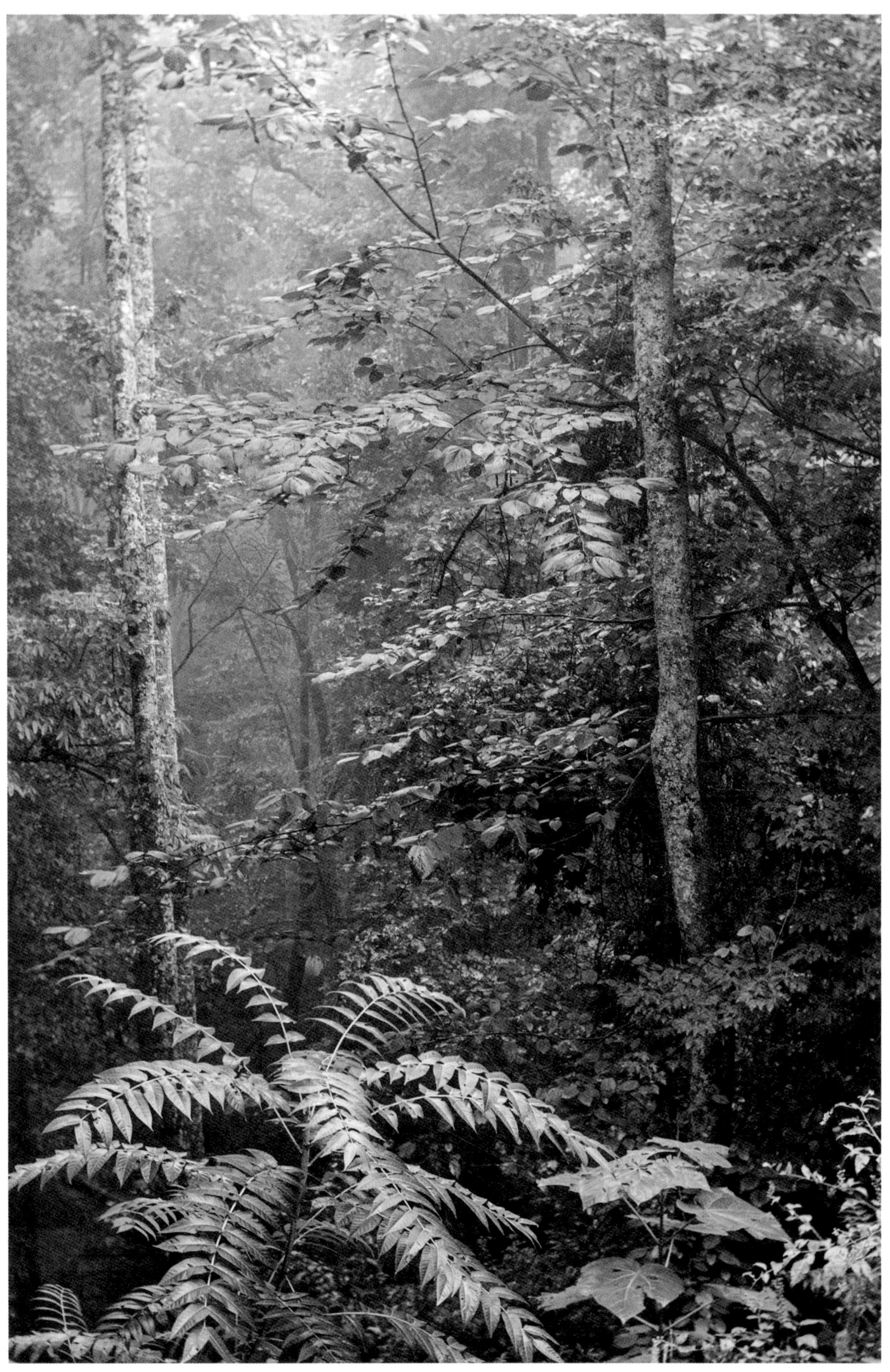

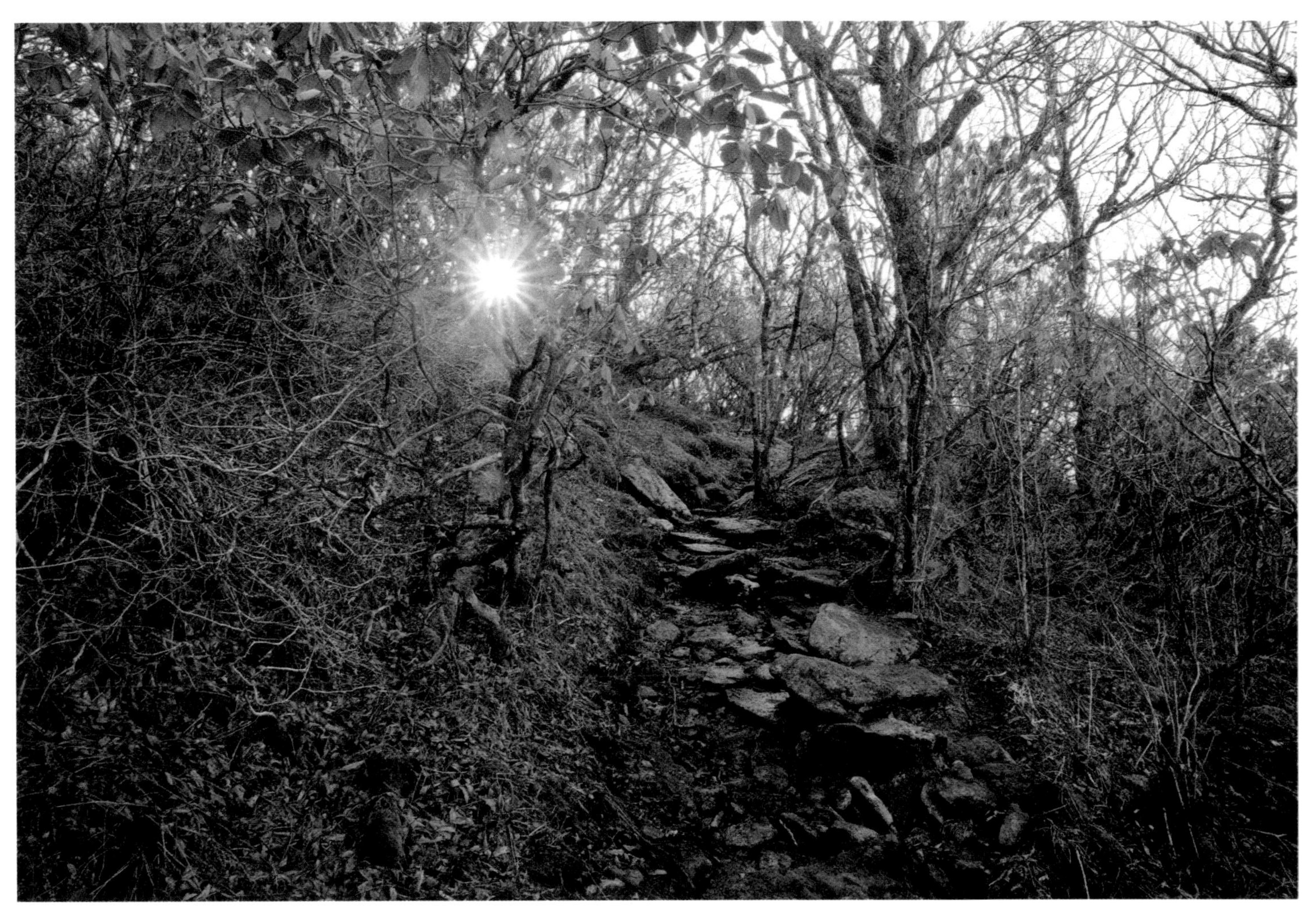

List of Plates

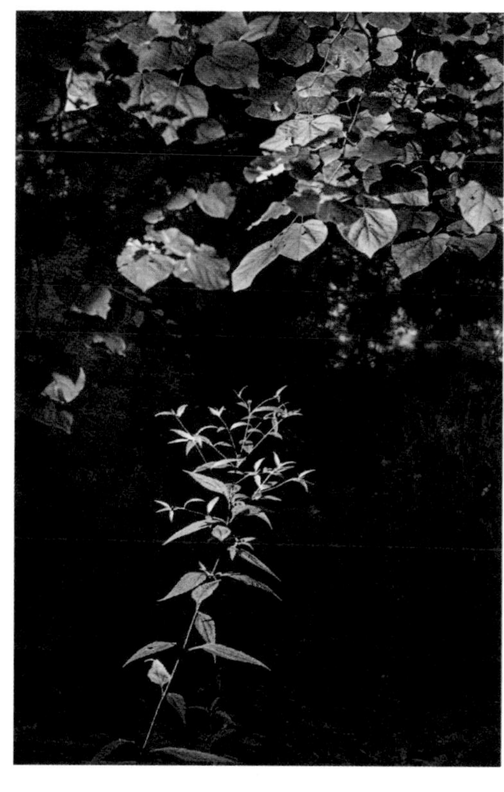

Afterword

I was inspired to begin this series of images during lockdown in the first Covid wave, when I was seeking to stay connected with life in a period of profound isolation. For four months, I took my elderly mother out of her congregate living facility and into my home to keep her safe before vaccines became available. At the same time, some family members and friends were seriously impacted by the pandemic both physically and mentally and also required my support.

Photographing daily on my mountain ridge and in nearby natural areas made and continues to make me feel more balanced and grounded. When I witness aspects of nature that have hung on through illness and physical harm, it gives me the strength to keep going. Nature heals my soul by reminding me how interconnected existence is, and how traces of energy remain and future growth is supported even after life-forms return to the earth. The often-lyrical way Mother Earth teaches us about the stages of life and death helps me live with what is happening to the planet and cope with mortality. Photographing ordinary things in my immediate environment taught me compassion for all living things, especially those that have been harmed or are different, as well as how to celebrate every stage of being, including the transition to nonexistence.

As I age, I find I am more interested in expressing my emotional response to the fragility and perseverance of nature, versus an idealized version of the environment. My images include traces of what was, things still hanging on, the effects of climate change and human impact, and the cycle of life, which includes decline and death, while also celebrating the commonplace, since all of life is precious. I am drawn to burls, scars, and other physical disconformities that evoke a history of experiences.

The magic of light is always a focus, whether it is how it can transform the ordinary into the extraordinary or whether it evokes the manifestation of the spiritual in the material. Shadows are important, too, as light would not be known without darkness and aspects of scenes that are not yet fully illuminated contain emergent possibilities.

Time is a unifying theme, because my photographs celebrate the present, while including elements such as roots that suggest the past, water, which is a continuum, and paths that serve as portals leading to a more hopeful future in these challenging times. In making these images, I strove to convey the lyricism of being and to create art that bypassed labels and my analytical mind and went straight to the heart of what is. Less increasingly became more, and explicative language began to feel inappropriate when attempting to describe why I was drawn to certain subjects. I began forming haiku in my mind as I was looking at the landscape before me. The idea for a book began to percolate.

The darkness of the times led me to switch from color to black and white, although I still photographed in color and then converted the images to black and white in post processing. Partway through the project, I decided that the shadows might contain the answers, or at least help define the questions, which are always more interesting. The everyday world became increasingly magical while I connected with the ground of being, as Heidegger described it almost a century ago. I began making digital negatives so I could make platinum-palladium prints and literally watch the images come into being as I exposed them to ultraviolet light and then submerged them in the clearing baths. Although additional prints can be made from the negatives, the process makes each one unique, as are the subjects they depict. The richness of platinum-palladium printing imbues darkness with its own beauty and the use of noble metals both preserves transitory states and underscores how valuable all of existence is despite, or perhaps because of, its impermanence.

—Lynne Buchanan

Acknowledgments

I wish to thank my mother, Barbara Berggren, who passed away while I was working on this book, for teaching me to care for our Earth and all life-forms and for showing me the importance of slowing down so I could see more deeply. I am also grateful for the lessons my deceased father, Douglas Berggren, taught me about ethics and the importance of living in right relation to nature. My father began explaining philosophy to me when I was a young child and never stopped questioning me about the nature of reality and what constitutes truth and meaning. Our discussions about aesthetics and the arts spurred my lifelong interest in synergies between the visual arts, literature, and music, and led me to earn graduate degrees in both art history and English, with a concentration in creative writing. I am also deeply indebted to Elizabeth Avedon, Elisabeth Aanes, and my fellow participants in the NORDphotography 2021 Photo Book Design Workshop for help with sequencing and refining my concept for the book. I would like to thank Jane Fulton Alt, Marie Bongiovanni, Carol Isaak, Emily Laux, Janet Matthews, Aimee McCrory, Denise Orlin, Sonja Rieger, Donna Spencer, Sandra Ullmann, Joan Lobis Brown, Julie Fischer McCarter, Leona Strassberg Steiner, and Sarah Thompson for their feedback and encouragement on this body of work. Without the teaching and support of Jill Enfield, I never would have started down the path of platinum-palladium printing; and I am forever grateful to Pradip Malde for mentoring me in the Malde-Ware printing-out process, which was the perfect method to make the images included in this book, since our time on this planet and what we see while we are here is both precious and transitory. My gratitude also goes to Pradip Malde for writing his profound and touching essay, and to James Lenfestey for allowing me to use two of his beautiful poems that set the stage perfectly for the rest of the book.

Thank you to the cofounders of Daylight Books, Michael Itkoff and Taj Forer. I am deeply honored to be included in their lineup of published artists. I am also indebted to the staff at Daylight Books, especially Ursula Damm, creative director, for her design expertise; Gabi Fastman, for her editorial work; and Sam Darby, for publicity and promotion. My thanks also go to my children, Jason, Azalea, and Carolyn Silverman for spending so much time in nature with me and reminding me to always see with fresh eyes; to Dave Halstead for his love and support and for being a wonderful hiking and life partner; and to John Buchanan, who provided encouragement and financial support while I was learning photography. Lastly, I am grateful to Mother Earth for allowing me to make a temporary home here and for helping me find meaning and connection. This book is a love poem to my family and nature, especially our forests, and is my way of returning the gifts that have been given to me.